HOLY GHOSTS

HOLY GHOSTS

Or How a (Not So) Good Catholic Boy
Became a Believer in Things That Go
Bump in the Night

GARY JANSEN

JEREMY P. TARCHER/PENGUIN
a member of Penguin Group (USA) Inc.
New York

JEREMY P. TARCHER/PENGUIN
Published by the Penguin Group
Penguin Group (USA) Inc., 375 Hudson Street, New York, New York 10014, USA * Penguin
Group (Canada), 90 Eglinton Avenue East, Suite 700, Toronto, Ontario M4P 2Y3, Canada
(a division of Pearson Penguin Canada Inc.) * Penguin Books Ltd, 80 Strand, London WC2R 0RL, England *
Penguin Ireland, 25 St Stephen's Green, Dublin 2, Ireland (a division of Penguin Books Ltd) *
Penguin Group (Australia), 250 Camberwell Road, Camberwell, Victoria 3124, Australia (a division of
Pearson Australia Group Pty Ltd) * Penguin Books India Pvt Ltd, 11 Community Centre, Panchsheel Park,
New Delhi—110 017, India * Penguin Group (NZ), 67 Apollo Drive, Rosedale, North Shore 0632,
New Zealand (a division of Pearson New Zealand Ltd) * Penguin Books (South Africa) (Pty) Ltd,
24 Sturdee Avenue, Rosebank, Johannesburg 2196, South Africa

Penguin Books Ltd, Registered Offices: 80 Strand, London WC2R 0RL, England

First trade paperback edition 2011
Copyright © 2010 by Gary Jansen

Most Tarcher/Penguin books are available at special quantity discounts for bulk purchase for sales
promotions, premiums, fund-raising, and educational needs. Special books or book excerpts also can
be created to fit specific needs. For details, write Penguin Group (USA) Inc. Special Markets, 375
Hudson Street, New York, NY 10014.

The Library of Congress has catalogued the hardcover edition as follows:

Jansen, Gary.
Holy ghosts, or, How a (not so) good Catholic boy became a believer in things that go bump in
the night / Gary Jansen.
p.   cm.
ISBN 978-1-58542-819-9
1. Jansen, Gary.   2. Haunted houses—New York (State)—Rockville Centre.   3. Catholic
Church and spiritualism.   I. Title.   II. Title: How a (not so) good Catholic boy became
a believer in things that go bump in the night.
BF1472.U6J36 2010   2010023072
133.1'29747245—dc22

Printed in the United States of America
1   3   5   7   9   10   8   6   4   2

ISBN 978-1-58542-895-3 (paperback edition)

Book design by Amanda Dewey

FOR MY MOM

It is generally supposed that amongst other restrictions Catholics are not allowed to believe in ghosts more than they are allowed to read an English Bible. This may be the popular belief, but incidents constantly break in contrariwise. Catholics, both priest and laymen, report ghosts or what are called "psychical phenomena." Many more notice them but say no more.

—*Shane Leslie's Ghost Book*

For the thousandth time, there's no such things as ghosts!

—Freddie Jones, *Scooby-Doo*

HOLY GHOSTS

BEFORE WE BEGIN

A few months before I became convinced that our Long Island house was being haunted by ghosts, I awoke suddenly in the middle of the night from a dream. For the first time in weeks, the night was quiet. I was in my bedroom. I was alone. My wife and our young son were sleeping at her mother's for a couple of days while I worked on a book I was writing. Moments ago, I had been sound asleep and now I was wide awake. I remember thinking to myself that I wished I woke up this alert every day for work instead of groggy and tired. Though the dream was startling—and, it turns out, unmemorable—I didn't feel afraid. On the contrary, I felt very much alive and aware of everything around me: the bed, the blanket, the air in the room, the temperature, the outline of the furniture, and the faint strips of streetlight streaming through a partially open blind. Everything in the room seemed to be breathing, and I felt a strange sort of union with everything around me.

As I looked around the room and listened to the night, I became very conscious of my body and the way my clothes felt against my shoulders and legs. I could feel the hair on my head and was aware of certain parts of my back, which seemed to press down more heavily on my mattress than others. I began to think about my skin and how it covered my entire body, that I was a landscape of ridges and curves. I then became very attentive of what lay beneath my surface: my bones and my organs. I imagined my heart pumping blood through my veins and arteries. I could picture my lungs expanding and contracting. I could see my stomach moving and digesting the food I had eaten earlier in the evening. I saw my liver and my kidneys cleaning toxins from my body. All of this activity was going on right below the surface of my skin and I tried really hard to listen closely to all of it, and you know what I heard?

Nothing.

Silence.

I couldn't hear my heart beating. I couldn't hear the acids in my stomach breaking down the food that was in there. I couldn't even hear my own breathing. I wasn't dead. This wasn't an out-of-body experience, it was a total in-my-body experience. I realized for the first time in my life that our bodies are really quiet, unless we're using our voices or experiencing a physical imbalance of some kind. Certainly, my stomach would growl from time to time or I would get a case of the hiccups on occasion, but those were exceptions. Most of the time, my body didn't make a peep (or at least not that I could hear). At that moment I became very aware that below my skin, less than an inch below the surface of my outer body, there was a silent, unseen world that was regulating and influencing my life all the time. It was, in many ways, an invisible realm, a place brimming with activity and energy, one that existed by its own rules and to which I was fully connected. It was also a world I had very little control over. Sure, I could change how deeply I was breathing or eat a food that would accelerate my heart rate, but I could never get my lungs to act like my pancreas. I couldn't get my brain to act like my esophagus. Each organ had its own function and generally lived in harmony with the others unless something was out of whack.

As I lay there thinking about these things, I asked myself: couldn't it be possible that there exists a world of spirits, an invisible world of ghosts, angels, and demons, one that is less than an inch away from our physical existence—a world that is mostly quiet (unless it's out of balance), acts by its own rules, and is just as influential and important in our daily lives as our own bodies are?

At the time, strange occurrences had been happening in my house, a classic haunting, if you will—odd noises, strange electrical anomalies, chills, objects moving of their own accord—and I didn't know how to answer my own question. When it came to an invisible world of spirits, all I could say was that I believed in God, and I had a difficult enough time believing in him, let alone a supernatural world populated by veil-like apparitions, Hallmark card cherubs, and little red men with pointy goatees and pitchforks. And even if a world like that did exist, what did it matter in my life?

I learned in time that it matters a lot.

THIS IS A BOOK about how I became a believer in ghosts, angels, demons, and the strange and unexplainable things that go bump in the night. As I am a devoted, albeit greatly flawed, Catholic and an editor and writer of religion and spirituality, this belief might not seem like much of a stretch. After all, almost all religions, including Catholicism, in one way or another begin with a supernatural event—"In the beginning God created the universe"—and their sacred scriptures from the Torah to the New Testament to the Koran to the Upanishads abound with stories of beings from an invisible world— some good, some bad—who either assist or wreak havoc on unsuspecting humans. Whether you are talking about the angels or devils—such as Michael, Satan, or the demonic *shedim* that surface in Christianity and Judaism, or the *djinn*, invisible and dangerous creatures made of smokeless fire in Islam, or the *rakshasa*, wandering night spirits in Hinduism, or the *preta*, the lost and hungry ghosts of Buddhism—religion has always talked of an invisible, and influential, world in the midst of our physical existence here on earth. For millennia, the unseen world was a very real world indeed.

But in modern times, where much of tradition has been pushed to the curb by technology, many of these beliefs have fallen by the wayside, considered by many, even within organized religion, as a useless vestige from an unenlightened and unscientific age. In turn, angels, demons, ghosts, and spirits have been relegated to the world of fairy tales, of metaphor, myth, legend, and superstition (and have made excellent fodder for novels, movies, and TV shows). Maybe this is a good thing. Certainly, a belief in witches and devils led to the death of thousands of individuals during the many European inquisitions the Catholic Church organized between the late twelfth century and the early nineteenth century. And to a lesser but still dramatic degree, right here in our backyard, Protestant Puritans executed twenty of their own—nineteen by hanging, one crushed to death by heavy stones—during the Salem witch trials of 1692–1693. In addition, though it's not a new concept, the political and superstitious act of "demonizing" one culture or society in order to carry out acts of slavery, terrorism, and mass murder, in many ways, defined the nineteenth and twentieth centuries and, unfortunately, continues to do so in our new millennium. It's no wonder that religion and a belief in what can't be seen or proven by empirical science continue to bear the blame for many of the world's problems (though when people ask me how could I be a Catholic with all the atrocities the Vatican has committed over its two-thousand-year existence, I like to remind them that it was three big atheists—Hitler, Stalin, and Mao, and not the Pope—who executed sixty million people in the duration of a generation). Who needs a ghost story when reality is frightening enough?

Up until recently, I never gave much thought to the spirit world. Like most people, the idea of a ghost or a demon was ancillary to my daily life. So were heaven and hell and what comes to pass after we die. I can't legitimately say I was a skeptic about these things—I had a number of unexplained incidents take place around me growing up—it's just that unless I was watching a scary movie or reading a Stephen King novel or attending a funeral, the thought of an invisible spirit (other than God) and a world populated by human-like beings with wings never really crossed my mind. And when it did, it never lasted long and I soon found myself focusing on more earthly pursuits, like paying my bills or checking the scores to see if the Yankees won. While heaven, hell, angels, and demons were basic tenets of my Catholic faith, they were never basic tenets of my life. Moreover, having grown up in and around the Catholic Church, I rarely ever heard a priest talk about spirits and such things, and these topics were never discussed during my twelve years attending parochial school. Sure, during church on Sundays a priest would occasionally whip out a fire-and-brimstone speech to scare us that the devil was a real person and not to be taken lightly, but most people just thought the man was having a bad day or was in need of some fiber. For me, and for most people in the pews, being a good Catholic (which I failed at more often than not) meant essentially doing the right thing. It was about maneuvering in a world that was seen, not in a world that wasn't.

All of this changed for me over the course of a single year, between 2007 and 2008, when unexplainable things began happening to me and my family on a regular basis in our home. I was thirty-seven at the time and my wife and I would soon welcome our second child into the world. Like many people my age, I was preoccupied with my job and responsibilities at home, like spending time with my loved ones and mowing the lawn. Also during this time, after years of struggling with my faith, I had made prayer a daily exercise in my life. The result was transformative—a sense of calm and focus I had never experienced before—and in many ways it was one of the most fruitful times for me spiritually. Each day was filled with the expectation of growing closer to God and in turn growing closer to the people in my life.

What I wasn't expecting was the discovery that our

house was haunted. Nor was I expecting to be drawn into an unseen world where ghosts weren't just the stuff of campfire stories, but dynamic, real things that could influence the world around me. Over the course of a year, my beliefs would be challenged and I would be forced to revisit events that took place during my childhood, leading me to once again reevaluate my faith. Moreover, I would encounter mind-boggling parallels between local history and events in my own family, and I would find myself engaging in a strange ritual to rid my home of ghosts. These bizarre events would forever change the way I looked at life, death, and what ensues after we say good-bye to this world. The experience was also a wake-up call to pay attention to the things I took for granted every day: loved ones, my thoughts, and, sometimes, the stupid words that came out of my mouth.

This book is a true story about my journey into the supernatural. Except where specifically noted to protect someone's privacy, everything is recounted as it actually happened. It is my hope in telling this story that it will help you to experience the world—the seen and the unseen—in a totally different way.

There is an invisible world out there and it is a very real world indeed.

PART I

Follow the Thread

There are more things in heaven and earth, Horatio,
than are dreamt of in your philosophy.
—*Hamlet*

The supernatural is real.
—Evelyn Waugh

L ate one night in the fall of 1996, I was walking through the narrow, fog-covered, cobblestoned streets of Prague in the Czech Republic. I was sort of homeless at the time, having recently been evicted from a friend's apartment after a silly comment I made escalated into a full-blown argument and a case of hard feelings. Trying to save as much money as possible before I hopped a train the next day to Krakow, Poland, I had opted not to spend the night in one of the city's many run-down hostels, where the walls were thin, the clientele high and obnoxious, and where you could catch gonorrhea just by looking at a doorknob. Instead, I had chosen a more hygienic alternative. I decided to walk the bridges and avenues of the city alone at night and if I needed to nap I would do so in a doorway or on the steps of a church or in the waiting room of the train station.

Though Prague was not as active as New York City, people were out in the streets at all hours of the night. Old Town, the most beautiful part of the *city for me, with its mixture of medieval, gothic, and baroque architecture, was alive with musicians, artists, and lost souls in search of someone to talk to. I could have used someone to talk to as well, but unfortunately, I didn't speak Czech. I was just another linguistically challenged American stray dog rambling through a former Communist country with an oversize backpack and a Eurail pass (which was worthless in any former Eastern Bloc countries at the time). Yet as I walked through the city, feeling a bit like a character in an Albert Camus novel, I was surprised to meet a few people who did speak decent English. I passed the time listening to their stories of haunted saints and lost lovers with wooden teeth, and their dreams of visiting America or moving to Japan to open an import-goods shop.*

One man, who smelled of wine and tobacco, pulled me aside, pointed to the sky, and told me that the atmosphere in Prague was different than in any other place in world, that if the clouds are just right, the color red turns black in the moonlight. He held up a red silk glove in front of me and told me to look carefully. I didn't have the heart to tell him it still looked red to me and that maybe, just maybe, he was color-blind. Instead, I told my newfound friend of my self-imposed exile, of my pursuit of God, that I had been stalking the Old Man for years and had tracked him down to this very place. He is evasive, I told him. But keep your eyes open, he could be anywhere. He just smiled at me and laughed. "You won't find God here."

I walked for most of the night between Old Town and New Town. Sometimes I would sit on the cobblestones of the Charles Bridge and stare at the statues of saints that lined the walls and wish they could talk and tell me what they had seen over the centuries—the lovers that strolled beneath the stars, the Nazis that crossed the bridge in tanks, the Russians, with their rifles and cigarettes. My feet hurt. I was tired and wild-eyed, and a little bit dehydrated from drinking Pilsner Urquell for the last twenty-four hours (which was cheaper to buy than bottled water and alleviated hunger), but eventually the morning arrived with no incidents and I watched the sun rise over the city, turning the streets from dark blue to miasma gray.

I had a few more hours to kill before I left for Poland, so I bought a roll and a cup of coffee somewhere. Afterward, as I was crossing the street near Wenceslas Square, someone hobbled and brushed past me, turned the corner, and then disappeared before I could get a closer look.

Prague was filled with pickpockets, and instinctively I touched the butt of my pants before remembering my wallet was in my backpack. At the time, I had always prided myself on being rather aware of my surroundings, but I hadn't heard him approach at all. I was startled and my heart was racing. I felt hot and flushed, and the ground beneath my feet felt spongy as if I were standing in mud. The street was quiet like the waking moments after your name is called in a nightmare, and I felt an intense desire to track whatever startled me and see where he was going. Since I had arrived in this land of cheap beer, beautiful women, schizophrenic architecture, dark fairy tales, and eerie-looking marionettes, I had been told, strangely enough by a number of travelers from Australia, to follow the thread. The world, they said, is a dark labyrinth and in order to find your way in life you have to follow the thread.

That was why I was there. I'd lost my way, was struggling with my faith, and as I looked around, these words flickered like an old movie reel in my mind. Standing there in the street, I felt the windows of the buildings staring at me with suspicious eyes and I became fully aware of how lonely and hungry I was. All I wanted to do was go home—my real home in New

York——but that wasn't happening any time soon. My plane ticket back to the States was nonrefundable and I couldn't make any changes. Plus, I was supposed to meet a friend in Paris in two weeks and I couldn't just leave her high and dry. Since my train to Poland didn't leave until around noon and with nothing else in particular to do that morning, I decided I would follow whatever it was that had incarnated itself in front of me. "Follow the thread," I said to myself, and turned the corner.

I soon saw a man in what looked like a ragged, headless bear suit, just some inebriated, limping circus performer who I was sure was on his way home to an angry, tired wife with a sharp pair of garden shears in her hands. I followed him for a couple of blocks until he unexpectedly went into a church, its façade blackened by years of Communism, soot, and dirty rain.

"What are you doing? You must be really bored to be following some old drunk," I said to myself and began to walk away when that still small voice in my head——which had gotten me into considerable trouble over the years——said I should go inside.

What the hell. So I did.

Ascending the stone steps, I opened the thick wooden door, entered, and stood in the nave. The church was quiet and dark, and a strong smell like burnt cabbage soup hung in the air. I heard faint tapping noises, the sound of heating pipes waking from hibernation. The man was nowhere to be seen. I was alone and, since I'm a sucker for old churches, I walked down the main aisle toward the altar, staring at the dark statues and the gold-colored buttresses and the stained glass. I listened to the sound of my footsteps echoing off the plastered walls and wooden pews and when I was just about underneath the hanging crucifix, I felt something touch my back.

I turned around expecting to see the man I followed into the church. But no one was there and I felt a strange heat break over me. I was all pins and needles and I looked down, thinking I had stepped on an exposed extension cord, but there was nothing beneath my feet except cold marble. Every nerve of my body was on high alert and my skin exploded into gooseflesh.

"Je-sus Chriiiiist," I said out loud, "what is that?"

And just like that, the feeling disappeared.

I turned around now and looked up at the ceiling and the colored windows and saw a figure of Saint Michael in the glass, wings unfurled, sword drawn, crushing the body of a demon. Then my eyes fixed on the large crucifix hanging above the altar and I stared into the eyes of the suffering wooden Christ and then whispered, "Are you there, God? It's me, Margaret."

There was no answer. Then something fell to the right of the sacristy. The crash scared the bejesus out of me and, not wanting to know what it was, I ran back up the aisle, out the door, and into the bright sunlight of morning.

Outside I looked around and saw no one. The street was empty and I instantly felt embarrassed and stupid. I also felt spooked and didn't know why. "Follow the thread, my ass," I said to myself. I quickly walked a few blocks, adjusted my backpack, and looked at my watch. Maybe I could get an earlier train, I thought and, dropping the proverbial thread in the street, I made my way across the city toward the train station.

Chapter 1

On a brittle winter evening in March 2007, I went to my three-year-old son Eddie's bedroom to get him a pair of socks. The night was cold and the room was dark except for a small night-light that cast a soft puddle of stars on the wall. Action figures and plastic toy blocks were scattered on the floor, and the bed was covered with folded laundry that needed to be put away. Wind was rapping the windows, and outside I heard a number of car doors slam almost simultaneously. This was not unusual. Our house is close to church, school, and municipal parking lots and there's always someone getting in or out of a car. That night, for some reason, I pulled the curtain aside and looked out the window. Across the street and down the block the lights of Macken

Mortuary, with its ornate Victorian-style gabled roof, burned brightly against an aubergine sky. I saw a small group of people in winter coats walking slowly to the corner, their bodies close together, their heads tucked low like pigeons warming themselves over a sewer grate.

I turned away, closed the curtain, reached into the dresser drawer, and felt something strange behind me, as if someone had been hiding in the shadows. There were only three people in the house at the time—me, my wife, Grace, and my son—and two of them were downstairs in the living room. I was startled, to say the least, as if I had been standing alone in a forest and heard a branch break behind me. My head jerked to the side and I quickly turned around, but there was no one there. I looked around the room, saw nothing unusual, shrugged it off, grabbed the socks, and as I was walking to the doorway I experienced something quite out of the ordinary—sort of like an electric hand rubbing the length of my back. I stopped and couldn't move, not because I was stuck but for the simple reason that the feeling was so strange. *What the hell is that?* The sensation then changed and I felt like I was being pressed like a grape, that something was coursing through my body like blood in my veins. Then the pressure seemed to break apart and for a brief moment I felt like I had a million little bugs crawling all over my back and neck. I raised my shoulders to my ears and tried to shake it off, and within seconds everything was back to normal. "Weird," I said out loud as I left the room and walked downstairs. And while what happened had been odd enough for me to take notice, by the time I handed the socks to Grace my mind was on other things. Namely, her.

TWO DAYS BEFORE, I had been at work when, by early afternoon, I suddenly felt like I was coming down with the flu. At the time I was editor-in-chief of Quality Paperback Book Club, a division of Book-of-the-Month Club, whose offices at One Penn Plaza sat above the netherworld known as New York Penn's Station—one of the busiest, and, with its bad lighting and cramped surroundings, most claustrophobic transportation hubs in the United States. I had been in meetings most of the morning and when I was in my office the phone was ringing off the hook. We were on deadline, and normally I would have just sucked it up and finished out the day, but I felt dizzy and feverish and, after talking to my boss in her office, I decided to leave early. I promised her I would make up some work from home that evening and went back to my desk, switched off my computer, and saw that the message light on my phone was blinking red. I ignored it. I walked downstairs in a bit of a daze to the train terminals, past midday travelers, the Andean flute player with a penchant for Celine Dion songs, and Tracks, an all-day-and-night purgatorial watering hole for commuters in various stages of weariness. I looked up at the digital departure board and saw I had two minutes to catch the next train. I made a run for it, my head pounding with each step. I descended to the platform, checked my cell phone, noticed I had a message but switched it off anyway, settled in on the train, and within a few minutes fell asleep during the forty-minute ride to Rockville Centre, a Long Island suburb twenty miles east of Manhattan and a place I've called home for most of my life.

MY GRANDFATHER used to say that every town and every rail line is haunted by tragedy. Rockville Centre and the Long Island Rail Road are no exceptions.

Charted in 1834, the Long Island Rail Road is one of the oldest rail systems in the United States. Today it is the busiest commuter railroad in North America, spanning approximately one hundred miles and stretching from as far west as Manhattan to as far east as Montauk. It serves, on average, eighty million passengers annually and the station at Rockville Centre is, like all stations on the Babylon Branch, on elevated tracks supported by a series of reinforced concrete pylons two stories high and two feet in diameter. This wasn't always the case.

After World War II, the population of the suburbs outside big cities like New York exploded with an influx of returning veterans. Grade-level rail lines, like the one in Rockville Centre during those years, ran flat to the ground and were seen not just as dangerous, but also as causes of congestion and traffic. In 1947, the decision was made to elevate the tracks on some of the branches, allowing cars and trucks to move freely across town. Temporary track lines were created during construction. On February 17, 1950, five months before the new platform was to be opened in Rockville Centre, a loaded eastbound train from New York traveling on one of the temporary tracks blew through a stop signal one block west of the station, colliding with a train traveling toward New York. The impact, which occurred at 10:43 p.m., sounded like a bomb going off. When rescuers arrived at the scene they saw broken, bloodied bodies, sometimes piled five high, amidst broken glass and twisted metal. The impact was so powerful, the head cars that collided were literally torn in two. Thirty-seven people died and 158 were injured. Doctors were forced to perform an amputation on one of the passengers in one of the destroyed trains. Local residents flooded the area in an effort to help the injured and to see if any of their loved ones were victims, but many were turned away by police because of the danger of the situation. Some just stood back and watched, others cried in the streets. Some walked to St. Agnes Church on Quealy Place a few blocks away and held vigil outside, offering prayers for the living and the dead being pulled from the wreckage.

My grandfather, who was obsessed with death, was the

first person to tell me the story of the crash. A broad-chested, strong-armed, big-bellied grave digger, with skin the color of autumn maple leaves, Harry George Powell worked for thirty years at Cypress Hills Cemetery in Queens, New York. He was a quiet man, with a macabre sense of humor when he spoke, and kept an unmarked tombstone by the head of his bed as a reminder that death was always inches away. Sometimes during the summer months, before I became a teenager, he and I would walk under the elevated tracks after we had bought a can of gas for the lawn mower he loved more than life itself and listen to the trains rumble overhead. In the heat of August, the great overpass would offer shade and, no matter how hot it was, there was always a cool breeze that would blow across your arms and neck. He had told me that when he first moved here in the 1960s, he would walk through this concrete alley and sometimes hear something like crying in the wind. During our excursions, we would stop and be very quiet and listen to the air, but I never heard anything myself. Years later, after I watched him die of a massive heart attack on the kitchen floor of his home while paramedics worked in vain to revive him, I would return to this area, hoping he might visit me there. As far as I know he never did.

GRACE, EDDIE, AND I were living in the house I grew up in, which was a half-mile from the scene of that accident, and on that winter afternoon in March as I walked underneath the train trellis on my way home from work—my head cloudy, my body chilled—all I could think about was getting into bed and going to sleep. As I neared our block, I could see my wife's car in the driveway. Grace, who was thirty years old at the time, was nearly two months pregnant and had been experiencing morning sickness the last couple of days. Her first pregnancy had gone without a hitch, and Grace—a strong-willed, fiery brunette who studied dance for years and rarely ever got sick—wasn't used to her body feeling the way it did. I hadn't talked to her since I left for work that morning, but she had told me that if she continued feeling nauseous she was going to call in sick.

During most weeks, Grace stayed home with our son in the mornings and worked afternoons at a local public school. Usually by this time of day, around 2:20 p.m., she would have been dropping Eddie off at his sitter's and then would have driven to her job. I felt guilty for not having called her and assumed she decided to stay home and rest. I opened the front door and heard a muffled call from inside. I walked into the living room and saw her lying on the couch, a small blanket wrapped around her shoulders, her arms tense and tight between her legs. She had been crying.

"What happened?" I had asked.

"Where were you? Why didn't you answer your phone?" She was angry.

Feeling like I was going to pass out, I apologized and told her I thought I was getting sick and asked if she was okay. She shook her head.

"No," she said. "I lost the baby."

MY WIFE GRACE grew up in a tight-knit, Catholic, Italian-American home in West Hempstead, New York, a middle-class neighborhood five miles north of Rockville Centre. Her father, Bert—whose interests ranged from physics and Greek mythology to collecting carburetors and watching 1950s B-movies—was an engineer, mechanic, and car enthusiast. On weekends he would restore old Fords and GTOs, and one of Grace's first memories is using an old air filter from her mother's 1969 metallic blue hardtop Mercury Cougar as a Frisbee. For most of her young life she lived with her mother and father, brother and sister, her aunt, her two cousins, and her native Sicilian grandparents in a split-level house. With ten people under one roof and daily visits from a contingent of relatives that all lived within minutes of one another, there was very little privacy and the place was never quiet. No one left home before they were married, and if you went to college you did so locally. But that suited everyone just fine. Family, more than anything else, was more important than personal freedom, individuality, or having a room of one's own.

But that family suffered a traumatic blow when, two weeks after her twenty-first birthday, Grace's father suffered a massive heart attack while at work at Con Edison, one of the largest energy companies in the United States, and one that supplies gas, electric, and steam service to New York City and Westchester County. He was forty-eight years old and was seen by all who knew him not just as an ideal father and husband, but as a generous, self-sacrificing man who embodied the ideal of serving others.

The family was, to say the least, devastated. Grace and I had been dating for a little over three years at the time and you could see in everyone's face shock mixed with despair and confusion. During those early days, family members had the tearful expressions of refugees exiled from their homeland.

Hundreds of people attended the wake and even more showed up for the funeral, which was held at St. Thomas the Apostle Church, a few blocks from their home. I was sitting with Grace in the pew during the Mass. She was crying, as was everyone around us, but at a certain point I looked at her and saw her eyes wide and clear. She was staring at the coffin that lay before the altar as the priest intoned prayers for the deceased and walked around blessing the area with a smoking thurible, a gold vessel suspended by a chain that contained incense. I followed her gaze and didn't see anything unusual. I thought she was just recollecting a fond memory or mentally shaking a fist at God for having let this happen to her and her family.

Later that day, she would tell everyone that she saw her father, as alive as the day, standing next to his coffin. He had stared at her and smiled and he looked like he did when she was seven years old and made her first Holy Communion: a full head of dark hair, tall and lanky with a thick mustache, and thick Coke-bottle eyeglasses. She couldn't believe her eyes and looked away for a brief second. When she looked back he was gone. To this day, she still regrets looking away.

Three days after the miscarriage, Grace was retelling that story to her mother and sister, who were sitting around the dining room table talking over tea and Dunkin' Donuts. I could hear her as I ascended the stairs to the second floor in search of Eddie's favorite book, *Goodnight Moon,* which had gone missing. It had been a long couple of days; I still felt sick and I was tired. I walked into my son's room, shuffled through Eddie's bookshelf, and felt the same strange feeling I experienced the night before crash over me like a heavy wave. My body felt like one giant electric surge. I tried to shake it off, but this time it lingered for about half a minute before disappearing as quickly as it came. "Seriously, what the hell is that?" I said out loud. I thought maybe it was chills brought on from a fever. I walked over and placed my hand on the radiator. It was lukewarm, so I bent down and opened the valve a half-turn. I went back to the shelf and eventually found the book, which had fallen behind a stack of old Hardy Boys mysteries. I went to the bathroom, took my temperature—it was slightly higher than normal—and walked downstairs, reciting to myself an altered version of Margaret Wise Brown's classic bedtime story:

> In the great green room,
> There was a telephone
> *And something really freaking weird.*

I didn't say anything to Grace or her mother or sister and quickly wrote it off in my mind as just a mixture of stress and feeling sick. After everyone left, I read Eddie his book on the couch and we all went to sleep early.

The following morning, a Saturday, I woke up at five a.m. and was feeling better. Whatever bug I had must have worked its way out of my system. At the time I was doing research for a book on prayer and was studying the *Spiritual Exercises of Saint Ignatius of Loyola*, a sixteenth-century Catholic mystic, who believed that since God created all things, then God was in all things. The duty of all people, then, was to seek the divine in all of creation. This idea appealed to me very much theoretically—but Grace's miscarriage was still in the forefront of my mind and I wondered where God was in all of this. I wasn't angry, at least, I didn't think so. I was just sad and perplexed.

. . .

FOR AS LONG AS I can remember, I have always felt drawn to God. Although I grew up in a religious household and had been Catholic all of my life—so much so that I thought for a time of becoming a priest when I was a teenager—it was only in my late twenties that I truly embraced my Catholicism. Part of it, I must admit, was an act of rebellion. Growing up, I had always felt like an outsider and by the time I was in third grade I made it a point to always reach out to the "uncool" kids in school. Friend of the friendless, I was. Well, for many people, being Catholic isn't very cool and for a time I used to see the religion I grew up in as a big goofy kid with braces and headgear. Even though I believed its heart had good intentions, modern Catholicism always seemed to be knocking its head against the wall.

Moreover, almost everyone I knew, from relatives to childhood friends to coworkers to people I met in college, were either atheists or agnostics. God, I believed, had been pursuing me for years, so I made a decision. As David Mamet wrote in his play *Glengarry Glen Ross*, "I subscribe to the law of contrary public opinion. If everyone thinks one thing, then I say, bet the other way." So I bet the other way and began to read the great theologians such as Saint Augustine and Thomas Aquinas and then modern spiritual writers like Thomas Merton and Henri Nouwen. I felt something stir inside of me and started praying the Rosary and soon thereafter started taking part in Penance and Communion, two Catholic sacraments, more frequently. I started attending Mass regularly and read the Bible every day. This is not to say I felt self-righteous or considered myself a moralist or that I didn't sin on a regular basis. On the contrary, I have told more than one priest during confession that I think a lot of people are assholes, including myself (but not you, Father!) and though I'm not really sure what commandment I'm breaking for this belief, it's been getting me into trouble ever since I learned that word (probably when I was five . . . thanks, Dad). Though I try to be a better person and do the right thing, my impatience and imperfections aren't going away anytime soon.

Mornings back then were my alone time with God—our talking sessions—and up until recently I had had the same routine for months. I would wake up early, go downstairs to the living room, read, pray, meditate, and write and after all that sit quietly and listen for a response from the Almighty. Most of the time I would hear nothing, but every once in a while, I would get an impression or a feeling of peace that would move over me or a thought would come to mind that, once followed, would lead me to an unexpected place. But listening for God after the miscarriage was difficult. My mind was racing with questions: Why did this happen? What are you trying to tell us? How could we have prevented this? I had been doing a lot of talking over the last couple of days and had received no response. In retrospect, how could I have ever expected to hear any answers when my mind was constantly fizzing over like Pop Rocks in a can of soda?

Not to mention that God speaks in a language more difficult than Portuguese or Mandarin or HTML. He speaks in silence. I remember saying *bullshit* the first time someone told me that, but I've come to realize that if you are still enough you can listen to silence like listening to music, you can read silence like reading a book. Moreover, if more than 80 percent of the way humans communicate is nonverbal, couldn't that mean that the majority of communication with the Divine is nonverbal as well? Prayer, meditation, listening—each was a tool for reading God's body language.

Of course, this isn't always an easy thing to do. That morning God had his arms folded, and everyone knows that's never a good sign. After a half-hour of sitting there and waiting for something, anything, I heard Eddie stirring over the baby monitor. I went to his room, sat with him on his bed for a minute, and then carried him downstairs. I gave him some milk and we watched cartoons until Grace came down a few minutes later.

She said she felt cold and asked me to check the heat and fetch Eddie a sweatshirt from upstairs. The thermostat read seventy degrees and the radiators were warm, so I walked upstairs and started rummaging through Eddie's drawers when the electric-like surge happened again.

And then it happened the next day.

And the next day.

And the next.

Whatever was transpiring in Eddie's room continued throughout March and into April and it seemed to occur only when I was in the room by myself. I continued to blame it on stress and soon threw weather into my list of explanations to myself. It had been a cold spring and, since the room only had a single window on a side of the house that didn't get much sun, I thought that seemed like a logical explanation. Still, something in my head was telling me it was something else. What that was, I just didn't know.

I hadn't told Grace about what I was experiencing. She was having a hard time after losing the baby and had been suffering from mild bouts of depression, a natural response to what she had gone through. In addition, Grace didn't seem to be experiencing anything out of the ordinary and neither did Eddie—I would watch their expressions when we were in the room and never saw anything unusual—so I just kept it to myself. And really, what was there to tell anyway? That the room was chilly or that someone with an electrified needle had a voodoo doll of me?

MY PARENTS had divorced in 1994, and though my mom received the house in the settlement, she hadn't felt at home there in a long time. She had rented it out for a while and tried for years to sell it, without success. Realtors brought potential buyers on weekends and after a short tour of the residence, everyone looked at each other and shook hands, but no one ever came back. While the old place may have been a little run-down—it needed a new coat of paint, the roof was old and weathered, and the kitchen, though clean and simple, was outdated and needed some work—it certainly wasn't a disaster. My mom tried different real estate agents and even dropped the price considerably, but there were still no takers.

Grace and I married in 1999 and lived in a small apartment—the first floor of a two-family house—on a little cul-de-sac in West Hempstead, not too far from her family's home across town. It was pretty and private and peaceful with a large backyard. Plus, our landlady, a little old Italian widow who lived upstairs, spent much of her time in Florida with her sister, so for most months out of the year Grace and I had the run of the place. It was in many ways a perfect setup for a newlywed couple.

But in the summer of 2001, my mom called me on the phone and asked if Grace and I would be interested in buying her house. The idea of buying a house, let alone the house I grew up in, hadn't crossed our minds. We were perfectly content to stay where we were, renting and not worrying about a large mortgage payment from month to month. My mom didn't pressure us, but I could tell from her voice that she was desperate to get the hell out of Dodge. For years she had wanted to start a new life in upstate New York, away from the congestion and memories of Long Island. She had recently found her dream home on the market—a small ranch that had once been used as a church in a hilly little town that straddles the New York and Connecticut border. But in order to move, she needed to sell the place she had lived in for most of the last twenty-five years. She just asked us to think about it.

We didn't have the money, and at first blush, I certainly didn't want to return to the place I had grown up in. Still, I always felt a little sorry for the house. From my earliest memories the place always seemed like it belonged on the Island of Misfit Toys along with Rudolph the Red-Nosed Reindeer. After a few days of talking it over, both Grace and I thought that maybe it wasn't such a bad idea. We were both interested in starting a family soon and Rockville Centre had great schools. Not to mention my mom's house was just a few blocks from the train station and it would cut my commute time by almost an hour every day. Maybe it was time to start thinking of buying and doing what grown-ups did. So we agreed that if we could get approved for a mortgage we would take a shot.

We applied, were quickly approved, and were supposed to close on September 11, 2001, but for obvious reasons we didn't. After a bout of rescheduling we became home owners two weeks later.

This was a bittersweet time for me. Though I fully knew what I was doing, I still felt a bit like this was a step backward. I was happy to be helping my mom and excited about starting a new part of my life with Grace, but kids were supposed to move away from home, not back into it. I was thirty-one and I felt like I was spiraling in reverse, plus the place was in need of a makeover, which was going to cost time and money. The only thing that saved me in those early days was Grace's reminders of the plan we came up with while we were eating scrambled eggs at a Greek diner at midnight a few weeks before: Buy the house, gut it, fix it up ourselves, and if we liked it, great, we'd stay. If we didn't, we'd sell it and go somewhere else.

In late September I started demolition. The first order of business was tearing up the floors, which for the most part were layers and layers of peel-and-stick linoleum tile. My mom was someone who got bored rather easily and she was constantly laying down new flooring every year, never bothering to take up the old, which meant that by the time I was fifteen we had about a full inch of gaudy plastic beneath our feet at all times. As I took to the floor with a flat-edged shovel, bits of tile broke apart, revealing all the different colors and designs my mom had experimented with over the years. Shit flew in all directions and I began reliving my childhood. I remembered the white tile with pink specks from when I was seven years old, the year I received not just my first Holy Communion, but hands down my favorite toy of all time, the Weebles Haunted House ("Weebles wobble but they don't fall down!"); the brown tile with fake gray grout from the time my five-year-old sister Mary fell on a toy, shattering it and in the process cutting her wrist; and the weird lemon-and-lime tile that looked like a bottle of Mr. Clean, which my mom put down a few months after tragedy struck our town in 1983.

ONE NIGHT IN MID-APRIL 2007, a little over a month after the initial incident in the house, Grace and I were downstairs at the dining room table. I was paying bills and she was sorting junk mail into two piles—tear (anything generic without our names on it) and shred (anything that had our names and personal information on it)—bemoaning the number of trees that were being cut down every year for paper and envelopes to advertise new cell phone plans and credit cards with introductory rates that skyrocketed to 75 percent interest after three months. Eddie was sleeping in his room upstairs and we could hear him stirring occasionally over the baby monitor receiver, which sat near the sink in the kitchen. From time to time this glorified walkie-talkie would hiss with interference. This was not uncommon. If one of us was wearing a sweater and sat down on the couch, it was enough to set off a nuclear explosion in its tiny speaker, akin to someone jacking up the volume on a television and then pulling out the cable antenna. That particular night, something different went down. As I was writing out a check and Grace was tearing glossy envelopes in two, we heard mumbling coming from the kitchen. At first we thought nothing of it. Not only does the monitor squeak with static, it has been known to pick up other people's phone conversations. Unfortunately, it's never anything terribly exciting. If something like that occurs, you want to hear someone admitting to a confidante that she is having an affair or you want to hear someone telling another person that they hid their mother up in an attic in order to keep collecting her Social Security check. Usually what we heard was more along the lines of "Did you go grocery shopping today?" "Yeah, I had coupons. I got lettuce."

But then the mumbling continued—a low, indiscernible voice. Grace asked if that was Ed and I wrote it off as just more static. But the sounds grew louder. Grace thought that maybe he was dreaming and decided to go upstairs and check. I went with her.

We opened the door to the bedroom and looked around, but we saw nothing unusual. Eddie was sleeping silently and we watched him for a few moments and he didn't move or make a sound.

Then we heard a faint low voice come from across the room.

Both of us stood still, forcing ourselves to be silent, and listened to the air. And then it happened again. This time we could tell it was coming from the bookshelf.

Now, the distance between Eddie's bed and the shelf is about seven feet, but that night those seven feet seemed like a mile. I walked over to the bookcase and there, peering down at us, was a stuffed Kermit the Frog doll, which let out a low rumbling sound like you would hear from a music box in slow motion.

We both stood still for a moment and I then reached up and took it off the shelf, its white eyes staring at me. I never realized how creepy something like this could look in the dark. I looked at Grace and she looked back at me, not scared, just puzzled. Neither of us even knew this thing made a sound but we quickly agreed that it must have had a dying battery in it.

Eddie began to stir in his bed and Grace and I tiptoed outside, closing the door behind us. In the light in the hallway I squeezed the doll, to confirm that it had a voice box. It did. So I turned it around and looked for a zipper, but there was no place to change the battery.

"Piece of crap," I said, trying to mask the fact that I felt a bit unnerved. Grace seemed unfazed by it all. As we walked downstairs, I thought I was just letting my imagination get the best of me, until the toy started speaking again in my hands.

I don't know if Grace saw the look on my face or not, but she grabbed Kermit from me and told me her brother could fix it.

I was spooked and I didn't really know why. I thought about the bizarre sensations I had been experiencing in Eddie's room and as I stood there looking at the toy sitting now on the dining room table I started to remember how this wasn't the first time odd things had happened to me. Nor was it the first time strange, unexplained phenomena had occurred in the house.

There was a long history I had tried to forget about, but I soon learned that some things you try to bury don't stay buried for long.

Chapter 2

One morning when I was a first-grader at St. Agnes Elementary School in Rockville Centre, New York, one of my schoolmates, a boy two years older than I was, told me a story I still remember, since it scared the hell out of me.

"Do you know the old, broken-down house on Lakeview Avenue?" he had asked me. "You know, the big one that's the size of the school? The one everyone stays away from?"

I told him I did.

"Well," he had said, "I heard from my sisters that the house is haunted."

He had my attention, but even as a first-grader I was a bit skeptical. I asked him how they would know.

He told me that the house was up for sale, and his parents and sisters had gone to look at it.

My skepticism eased a bit. This was not unlikely. My family, too, had looked at the house before they'd settled on a smaller, even more run-down place across town.

The story he had heard from his sisters, and was passing on to me, was that there had been a very unhappy man who lived there and had done horrible things to kids.

I asked him what kinds of things, but he didn't know. His sisters wouldn't tell him, but they must have been really terrible. One day, according to this boy, the man felt so guilty about what he had done that he hanged himself in the bathroom.

Now, *this* was possible. I had been with my parents when they were looking at that house and it had the creepiest bathroom I had ever seen: dark blue walls, a tiny, dirty window that let in only the faintest light, exposed pipes, and a toilet with an overhead watershed and chain you had to pull to flush. The chain had reminded me of the cord the Addams family always used on TV to summon Lurch from whereabouts unknown. I had never seen anything like that before. As he continued telling me the story, I imagined some old guy with his tongue dangling from his mouth, hanging from a pipe, his feet inches above the place where moments before he had dropped a deuce.

But all I said was, "Really?"

"Snapped his neck!" he replied.

I told the kid what Father Bennett had said in church one day: you're not supposed to kill yourself; if you do, you will go to hell.

The boy continued telling the story and I was listening with rapt attention when a Polaroid flash of disbelief went off in my head.

"The owners told your parents this?" I asked. I was pretty sure, even in my seven-year-old mind, that I was probably being set up. If you're trying to sell a house the last thing you want to tell someone is that some creepy guy was found hanging above a crapper.

"No, stupid," my schoolmate said, "My sisters heard from their friends at a slumber party." That made more sense to me. I was satisfied by that response. Maybe he was telling the truth.

There was more to his story. Supposedly, the man who killed himself still walks around the halls with the noose around his neck. He moans and knocks things down. That was why the owner wanted to sell the house. To get away from the guy with rope.

"And you know what?" he had asked me.

"What?"

"They say he has another piece of rope in his hands looking to hang his next victim. And you know what else?"

"What?"

"He's been looking for you." And on the very last word, he reached out, hollered, and grabbed me by the neck.

I remember screaming. His hand was pinching my skin and I wasn't able to breathe. I pushed him off, called him an asshole, and ran. I could hear him laughing as I took off. I didn't want him to know it—I'm a bit ashamed to admit it even now—but he almost made me pee my pants. I held it in, though. When you're seven years old, one of the last things you want to do in school is wet yourself. I, for one, never wanted to be known as Gary "Piss His Pants" Jansen.

His story rattled me. All day long I waited for dismissal, my leg bouncing up and down in my gray uniform pants, just so I could go home and tell my mom about the incident at school and ask her if ghosts were real and if they could kill you.

I was kind of an innocent and credulous kid at the time and I was still getting used to being in school. My mom had never sent me to kindergarten, opting instead to keep me home during that oh-so-important first year of primary education. Even though my mom worked most days, she hadn't been ready to give up her firstborn son to people (teachers) she didn't know, so my sisters and I would hang out in my grandparents' house. Trust, when it came to people outside of the family, was in very short supply.

But staying home was fine by me. Like most kids, I didn't want to go to school anyway. I much preferred watching *The*

Young and the Restless with my grandmother and getting into bits of juvenile tomfoolery with my younger sisters (which always seemed to involve kitty litter, brown paper bags, and Barbie dolls). So, instead of sitting in a boring classroom, learning about Jesus, reciting my ABCs, learning how to cut with safety scissors, and how not to eat paste and not jam sharpened pencils in my ears, I learned how to read and write—and I learned about life—from watching *Sesame Street* and *The Electric Company* in the mornings, soap operas during lunch (after *The Young and the Restless* aired at 12:30 p.m. came *Guiding Light*), *The Magic Garden,* a half-hour educational show that took place around a large tree and featured hippie chicks Carole and Paula and their orangey-pink giant squirrel, Sherlock, at 2:30 and then *Casper the Friendly Ghost* at three o'clock every weekday.

Television. My friend, my classroom.

Of all the shows at the time, *Casper the Friendly Ghost* had the greatest impact on me. It still makes my heart race. Why? Did it scare me, you ask? *Au contraire, mon frère*; I *adored* that show. *Casper* was a delightful cartoon about a cute little ghost who was always trying to do the right thing, even though his uncles, the Ghostly Trio, tried their damnedest to wreck the poor dead kid's quest to make friends. To this day it brings back memories of sitting in my grandfather's musty old La-Z-Boy chair, drinking RC Cola, eating pretzels and potato chips. Watching with me would be my purple-haired grandmother (she dyed her hair every month and, for reasons unknown to me, her attempts at staying brunette always ended up with her looking like an eggplant) or, sometimes, my mom, if she was home in time from work.

That show resonated for me in a way that no other show did at the time. Maybe it was because I was a lonely little kid in search of friends, despite the fact that I loved being home. Maybe I just liked the idea that ghosts could be friendly little cherubs with cute laughs and transparent hearts of gold. And that they couldn't hurt you.

Whatever the reason, that show was my first introduction to ghosts and to the idea that there could be an unseen world in our midst.

WHEN WE WERE DISMISSED at 2:40, I raced to my grandmother's house right across the street from the school, switched on *The Magic Garden,* and waited for my mom to arrive from work and take me and my sisters, Julie and Suzie, who were four and two years old at the time, home. We lived nearby, just a short walk across the school parking lot. I went back and forth between watching Paula and Carole reenacting the story *Caps for Sale* on TV to glancing at the wooden cuckoo clock that never cuckooed above the living room couch. Minutes seemed to last for hours as I kept thinking of the man with the snapped neck walking around that old house calling my name. While I was pretty sure that my schoolmate was full of shit, I still had my doubts.

I kept thinking back to the day my family and I had been there. Had the ghost been there as well, hiding in a dark corner, waiting for me, ready to throw the noose over my head and hang me from a doorway?

Eventually my mom arrived, harried and rushing to get us home so she could cook dinner for my dad. As we were walking to our house, I told her what the kid had said.

"Don't listen to him," she said. "I didn't feel anything when we were there." This made me feel much better, so I asked, "Are there such things as ghosts?"

She didn't answer. I asked again and all she said was, "Let's get going. Your father will be home soon." This was not the first time I had asked her this question. I had done so pretty much from the time we'd moved from my grandmother's into our own house across the way. Why? Because our new residence was always making noise.

Built in 1904, the old Colonial was prone to drafts and creaky floors. The rooms were usually cold. These things were true for as long as I lived there. We moved in in 1976. I was six years old at the time and had no idea that the place had a notorious reputation. It was known as a hippie commune, a place where local kids in tie-dye and bell-bottoms came to party and do drugs on a regular basis. The previous owners had rented the house to their son, a college student, and there was a sort of "Don't ask, don't tell" agreement between them. Parties occurred frequently, and many times my grandmother would see police lights flashing outside her window at all hours of the night.

My mom and dad had married in 1968 and had been living with my mother's parents for nearly eight years, and by 1976 they were ready to move. Earlier that year, my mom was coming home from work when she found a piece of crumpled newspaper in the backyard. She opened it and circled in red was the classified listing for the house across the parking lot. She saw this as a sign from God and she soon convinced my father to go and have a look.

The house was a mess. The rooms, many of them with garbage and stained mattresses on the floor, were painted fluorescent orange and pink and red. There were flower and star decals stuck to the walls. The place smelled terrible and in the front room of the house was a hundred-gallon aquarium tank that, my parents had been told, housed a fifteen-foot boa constrictor. My father, an upholsterer, was a working-class Joe and a big anti-hippie and would sometimes walk by the house at night and see "college boys" sitting on the lawn, smoking and playing guitar while the giant snake rested calmly on the laps of their girlfriends.

My dad hated the place. My mom, however, saw past the disaster inside, past the crumbling plaster and loose flooring. She saw a place she could make a home. Eventually, she was able to convince my dad that the house was a good idea. My father wasn't too excited to be living next door to his in-laws, especially after having lived so many years in their house, but a deal with the owners was eventually struck. My parents would rent the house for at least one year with an option to buy at a later date. My mom was over the moon and, though my two sisters and I were spooked about the inside, we were ecstatic about the huge backyard. There was ample space to play and three giant-size elm trees, so, for us, it wasn't just a private park—it was our very own forest.

My parents spent months cleaning the place, throwing out old furniture, broken bongs, and moldy magazines. Though I wouldn't learn this until years later, my mom also found a box filled with tarot cards, a Ouija board, and strange books that creeped her out and were quickly discarded. They spent their nights painting the kitchen and bedrooms, laying carpeting and nailing dark wood paneling to the living room and dining room walls. (That was the style back then, but really, what were they thinking?) By the time we officially moved in, my parents had transformed the old place into a rather cozy little home for a young family.

But the house was always cold and, like Rice Krispies, would snap, crackle, and pop on a daily basis. At night you would hear what sounded like tapping behind some of the walls. We were told not to worry, that it was just the plumbing. At other times we would hear creaking on the hallway stairs as if someone were walking up and down. Again, we were told not to fret, that the wood was just expanding and contracting because of problems with the heating system.

My dad had a practical explanation for everything. Like Grace's father, he was a jack-of-all-trades and the master of the Rube Goldberg repair. He could fix anything and prided himself on mending cracked car mufflers with a tin can and a wire coat hanger, and leaky water pipes with Silly Putty and rubber bands. My parents eventually bought the house. I think my dad had come to see it as one giant challenge to his wits and creativity. And though he had many successes, including installing new sinks, new toilets, and new kitchen cabinets, he never seemed to have much luck with the damn heat. This went on for years. Every fall as I got older, he and I would bleed the cast-iron radiators that sat like giant accordions in the corners of each room. For a couple of weeks, the house would feel warm and comfortable. But as soon as the days and nights turned really cold in December, usually right before Christmas, the furnace would inevitably break down. On any given morning, you could find my mom and my sisters and me huddled around an open oven trying to stay warm, with my father cursing away in the basement.

On one occasion, my mother had put water up for tea. I was warming my back while she was in the other room getting my sisters ready for school. I must have moved too close to the lit burner because my undershirt caught fire, the flames riding up my back. I had no idea anything was wrong until I saw my mother run in from the other room, her arms flailing. She knocked me to the ground and started smacking my back with her hands. I tried pushing her off me but she was too strong. I smelled something like burning paper and yelled out. She yelled too and I still wasn't sure what was going on. When it was all over, my charred shirt fell off around me. Its entire back had been fried. I was fine and so was my mother. She told me the flames had reached to the ceiling and when we looked up there was a black mark above where I had been standing. Not one part of me was burned, not my neck, not my hair. My mother called it a miracle and when I thanked her for what she had done, she told me to thank the angels who had protected me.

After that, the stove, as a means for heat, was off-limits.

FOR A SHORT TIME, the tapping behind the walls went away, but new noises seemed to take its place. On a regular basis we'd hear what sounded like footsteps walking across the attic when no one was there. Occasionally, a loud bang would ring through the house for no apparent reason, as if a small army had slammed into one of the rooms. The noise never sounded like it was coming from outside, always inside. And the staircase would continue to creak throughout the night. "It's an old house," my father would tell us. "It's going to make noise." Then with a touch of disgust in his voice he would add, "Plus, you got *all that* going on out there." *All that* referred to the daily traffic that was then, and still is, a part of life in our little section of town.

Businesses have come and gone, and the façades of store-fronts have changed repeatedly over the years; even the green wooden "Monster" fence at Hickey Field, where I hit my first and only home run as a Little Leaguer, has been replaced with cold impersonal chain link, and most of the kids I played with are all grown up and living lives in new places far away from here. Still, Rockville Centre hasn't changed much in the last thirty years. A suburb on the south shore of Long Island, twenty miles east of Manhattan, the town is a mostly quiet, mostly picturesque, family-friendly neighborhood with big houses, tree-lined streets, and manicured lawns. Our house, however, resides in a commercially zoned area of the village, where grease pits, delis, bars, and a variety of small businesses—from barbershops to printers to a locksmith to a hobby store that still sells model airplanes—are part of the local land-scape. On weekends and during summer vacation, the area is a magnet for teenagers with limited imagination and not much to do. You don't find much graffiti in Rockville Centre, except near us.

Our block was also what some people called an "artery to Catholic town." Across the street from our house sat St. Agnes Elementary School, where my sisters and I attended class for eight years. Next to that was the family-owned Macken Mortuary, *the* place for Catholics to be laid out when they kicked the bucket. Adjacent to the funeral home was St. Agnes High School, separated by an asphalt walkway from the grand cathedral, which became the seat of the Catholic diocese of Long Island in 1957, seven years after the train crash a few blocks away.

If you lived on the east side of town and had to get to one of those places, you most certainly used our block to get there. It was not uncommon to hear commotion outside: students making noise during the day, churchgoers gossiping on weekends, drunks moaning and throwing up near the telephone poles, or the sounds of strange voices arguing in the middle of the night. Nor was it uncommon to catch kids smoking pot or a couple screwing in a car.

During the day my father labored in the workshop at Tri-Art Breakfast Nooks, a kitchen furniture store on Sunrise Highway, less than a mile from home. In the evenings he would deliver the chairs and tables he created and assembled all year round to customers on Long Island and in the five boroughs. He would sometimes work as late as nine o'clock making deliveries, and when he would lose daylight he would shine a heavy-duty spotlight on customers' homes in order to locate the exact address.

"Rich people always have the tiniest numbers and they almost never turn on their outside lights," he would complain. "How the hell am I supposed to deliver this shit if I don't know which house is theirs?" Little did I know at the time that my father's rants were my first foray into the world of American class differences.

When I was young I would occasionally accompany him in the evenings. When we'd arrive home after these jaunts, there would often be unsuspecting lovers tucked away in sweaty little Subarus and cramped Volkswagen bugs, hidden in the shadows of the parking lot near our house. My father would pull out the old spotlight, lean over the fence, and shine it on the couple. When I say spotlight, let me be more specific: it was 10,000 candlepower. In fact, he'd always warned me never to beam it into anyone's eyes, though I did it to myself on numerous occasions. Anyway, thanks to Dad, I got to see my first naked ass.

"What are you doing?" he'd half yell, half laugh to them. Then we would see sudden movements behind the windshield. Seconds later, the headlights would flick on and the humiliated couple, blue-balled and half dressed, would peel out of the lot, never to be seen again. My father, while quite the comedian, wasn't what you would call a romantic.

My mother, on the other hand, *was* a romantic—the polar opposite of my dad. The only thing that they seemed to have in common was their youth. They were married when they were sixteen and seventeen, respectively. He was Lutheran, pragmatic, and a realist. She was Catholic, idealistic, and a dreamer. Mom was a bit of a suburban mystic. She saw and knew things that other people didn't. As a little girl she had a vision of Jesus standing in a doorway moments before she learned of the death of her beloved grandfather. "He looked kind," she said. She took that vision as a sign that she should give her life to God. Two nights later she had another vision, but this time it wasn't of Jesus. She was stirred from sleep by the feel of someone sitting on her bed. When she opened her eyes, her grandfather was there smiling at her. She stared at him for a few moments and then reached out to touch him and he faded away.

Visions weren't anything new in her family. Her mother, Julia McGreevy Powell, who worked for more than twenty years as a butcher in various A&P supermarkets on Long Island, had visions of Jesus on five separate occasions throughout her life. Like my mother, she saw these occurrences as signs that she was being called to live her life in a convent. My grandmother, a feisty Brooklyn native who loved to tell stories about Coney Island and Ebbets Field and reminded everyone, practically on a daily basis, that she thought Frank Sinatra was a snake, would have none of that. She married, some would say, just for the sake of getting married. Her husband, my grandfather, had served under Pierre Salinger in the United States Navy during World War II and tumbled from job to job until finally settling in as a grave digger, where the work was relatively quiet and solitary. My grandmother liked to talk. My grandfather didn't and they never really got along. Still, they had three children together and the unhappiness that followed was never blamed on my grandmother's decision to pick an incompatible spouse, but on her refusal to become a nun. "God," she would say, "ain't nothing but hard luck."

My mother never believed that. She loved God and would pray every day, sometimes seated in empty churches, staring at the stained glass and the crucifix that always hung above the altar. For a while she dreamed of becoming a nun, of devoting her life to God, whom she loved more than anyone in her life. Yet when she was fifteen she met the young man who would become my father (he was sixteen) and a year later the two of them were married before either was old enough to vote. Both sets of parents were against the decision at first. But while my father's side grew colder and colder, my mother's parents quickly learned to embrace the tall, wiry boy, eventually taking him into their tiny, barnlike house. Their wedding ceremony was small. Only my mother's parents showed up. But it was, as my mother said throughout the years, all part of God's plan. What that plan was (and she would allude to it many times while I was growing up), she never really told me. I was born a year later and my sister a year and a half after that. Three more sisters followed over the next ten years.

My grandparents never had much money, and my parents were very poor in those early years. My sister Julie and I lived with them in my grandparents' tiny unfinished basement, parts of which had a dirt floor, not to mention exposed water and sewer pipes. I had a lot of nightmares growing up there, but my mom was always there to reassure me that everything was all right, that there were always angels watching over me, and not to be afraid.

FIRST GRADE CAME AND WENT, and my childhood tastes matured. Soon after, I left behind Casper, his best friend, the cute little blonde witch Wendy, and their trusty white-haired spectral colt, Nightmare, for a more grown-up, much more skeptical (yet still animated) take on the supernatural. That's right, *Scooby-Doo*. Here was a totally different look at the world of ghosts and monsters. Even though Casper would always hold a special place in my heart, Scooby and the gang— goateed Shaggy, ascotted Fred, nerdy Velma, and the desirable Daphne (I have a crush on her to this day) with their Mystery Machine and scientific, albeit far-fetched, approach to solving crimes—would instill in me two very important ideas: one, there are no such things as ghosts; two, if you looked hard enough, there is always a logical explanation for things that go bump in the night.

With all the noises going on in our house, these ideas turned out to be therapeutic, and I would repeat them to myself when I felt afraid. And if *Scooby-Doo* episodes were not enough to convince me that spooks were just in your imagination, Catholic school most definitely was. The nuns, priests, and teachers drilled into us during religion class that God was good, that Jesus saved us from our sins, and that there was only one ghost—the Holy Ghost, the Holy Spirit. There was no talk of ghosts or specters, or angels or demons, for that matter.

As a result, the reassuring Scooby-Doo mantras became infallible truths in my young life. They came in especially handy when my family and I would continue to hear unexplained noises in the night: the shuffling of feet upstairs when no one was there; the staircase creaking on its own, as if someone were sneaking around and listening to our conversations; the faint indiscernible whispers we'd hear while my sisters and I played with our toys; the ringing of the doorbell in the middle of the night and no one being there; the sound of breaking glass when there was no evidence of a broken window or dropped plate or bottle anywhere.

And while I quickly became sure that there were no such things as ghosts, and that everything had a logical explanation (chanting this mantra over and over again), not everyone in my family was convinced.

ONE NIGHT IN THE FALL OF 1977, my mother told me during dinner that there was a ghost in our house. I was still seven years old, and we were sitting at the kitchen table. It was just the two of us. My father was away on a hunting trip, and my sisters were in the living room watching TV. I was always a slow eater and Mom was keeping me company at the kitchen table. What I remember most aren't the words she said, but the rubbery texture of the pork chops I was eating. It was a little like trying to eat old, chewed gum—flavorless—and no matter how much you chewed or how much saliva you excreted, the pork pieces never broke down enough for easy swallowing. My mother was convinced that one of us was going to die of trichinosis, so she boiled all pork products until they were the color of dirty laundry water. Botulism from dented cans was another concern. Since our family didn't have a lot of money at the time, what we ate was mostly of the half-price dented can variety. I had once heard on the nightly news that the contents of a dented can could mean sure death. I would envision drowning in a pool of my own vomit, and that image, not some ghost, scared the shit out of me.

Meals in our house always felt a little like a last supper; creamed corn, lima beans, glazed carrots, all chambered bullets in the fatalistic game of dinnertime Russian roulette. On more than one occasion my mother reassured us that she could cook the bacteria out, but I was always skeptical. After each bite I took I would wait a minute to see if I was going to die.

Back to my mother and me, alone at the table. "What did you say?" I had asked between horse chews of pork.

My mother, who loved her velvet Jesus pictures and old Hayley Mills movies, did not fool around. With a serious look on her face, she took a drag of her cigarette and a sip from her cup of tea.

"There's a ghost in our house. She's in the front room." She said these words matter-of-factly, as if she had said, "Today is Wednesday" or "Your aunt is on drugs" or "Your grandfather buried them three deep last weekend."

"You can see a ghost?"

"No. I can feel her. She leaves an impression on me. She likes to stand by the picture window in the front room. It's as if she's looking for someone."

I didn't know what she was talking about. "Should I be afraid?" I asked.

She said no. Maybe it was her deadpan, surgical delivery, or maybe I was more focused on how in God's name I was going to finish my food without throwing up on the table, but I didn't feel afraid. I never felt afraid around my mother. I can't say I believed her at the time nor can I say I disbelieved her. There was no reason for my mom to make up the story. She wasn't trying to scare me and she never talked about it much. Only on occasion, over the years, would she mention the ghost in our house, reminding me that the woman was just lonely and since she wasn't causing anyone any trouble there was no need for us to cause her any trouble either.

. . .

MY MOTHER was a very sensitive person, not just emotionally (though she was known for crying at the drop of a hat while watching Fred MacMurray movies), but in other ways, too. She knew when it was going to rain and when it was going to snow regardless of what the weatherman said. She claimed to feel souls of the departed in church, but not in cemeteries. And long before there was caller ID she was able to tell you who was calling before you answered the phone.

And then there were her dreams. They were dreams of lost kittens and dogs who would show up days later on our front stoop like shipwrecked sailors in search of dry land. My mom took many of these wandering animals into our home temporarily, but not every stray was given sanctuary. Sometimes angels come to our door, she would say, sometimes *something else* comes to our door. We let the angels in. We don't want the *others* in our house. What that *something else* was and how she knew the difference, she never said for sure. *It's just a feeling I get*, she would tell me.

As I was growing up I always enjoyed being with my mom and listening to her stories. But I just didn't share her enthusiasm, her belief in an unseen world of ghosts and angelic and demonic forces. This was probably because I felt that nothing weird ever happened to me, except for the noises in our house, which never went away but became so familiar that most times you would forget about them. Even when the house would seem to be doing something funky, I, like my father, was a rationalist. Everything had a reasonable explanation. What those explanations were, well, we never knew. And I didn't really care. It was hard to convince me of anything, even when my mom's gift for seeing things others did not see proved to be prescient and terrifying.

LATE ONE NIGHT in March 1983, when I was thirteen years old, I heard my mother crying downstairs. My bedroom was on the second floor. I had been sleeping but woke up to go to the bathroom. On my way back, I could hear the sound of whimpering. All the time I was growing up, both my parents were hotheaded and fought on a regular basis. The sound of yelling or crying wasn't anything unusual. But what was strange about this instance was that, as far as I knew, there had been no argument. I often woke up when they started to yell, but that night, except for the sound of faint sobbing, everything was quiet.

I walked downstairs to see what was wrong. There was my mother, sitting in the dark in the front room, smoking a cigarette and staring out the large picture window that overlooked our block and the VFW Hall across the street. Also visible was the spire of St. Agnes Cathedral a short distance away, silhouetted against the night sky. She was sitting on an old chair in an upright fetal position, knees tucked under her chin, and she was crying. In her left hand was the faint, orange glow of her cigarette, and in her other hand she held an old plastic ashtray. I'm not even sure if she saw that I had walked into the room.

I whispered to her, asking what was wrong. At first she didn't respond. It seemed as if she was in a trance. I moved closer to her and whispered again. I felt afraid, not of my mother, but of the situation. Maybe she was sick.

She took a drag of her cigarette and just sat there, rocking back and forth slightly in the chair. Her hair was pulled back behind her ears. My dad had always said that she looked like a little girl when she did that, and for a brief moment I felt as if our roles were reversed. She had always asked me what was wrong, had always reached out to me, had always tried to make things better; now I wanted to do the same.

Once again I asked her what was wrong. She took a deep breath in and as she did, tears started running down her face. Quietly, she cried out these words: "The light in the church has gone out."

That's it? I thought. *She's crying because the bishop forgot to pay the electric bill?* I stood there in my pajamas, a bit relieved, a bit perplexed. I waited for her to say something else, but she didn't. She did, however, start to hyperventilate, and I asked her if she needed a bag. She nodded.

Every once in a while, usually after arguing with my dad,

my mom would lose her breath and she'd need to breathe into a brown paper bag. I never understood how that would make her feel better. Nonetheless, I dashed off down the hallway to the kitchen, found a bag and raced back to her. I opened it, rolled it down a bit, handed it to her, and watched the bag expand and contract like an external lung.

I stood there, confused by what was going on. I thought for a moment about getting my dad but decided against it. I looked out the window, down the block toward St. Agnes, and she was right, the light at the very top, just below the iron crucifix, had gone out. Though I had seen the church when I first walked into the room, I hadn't noticed how dark it looked. It did seem a little strange, since for as long as I could remember that light was always on. Regardless, why was this upsetting my mother?

When she was done breathing into the bag, she looked a little more like herself. I asked her again what was going on, why was she so upset?

"It's a bad sign," she said. "*They* are telling me something terrible is going to happen."

I asked her who *they* were? And she didn't respond. I asked her what she was talking about.

"Something terrible is going to happen to someone close by. Someone is going to do something horrible."

Up until then I had never felt frightened by anything

my mom said or did. That all changed in an instant. I stood there, feeling as if my legs had turned to tree stumps, with thick roots grown into the floor. I wanted to turn around and run back upstairs, but my mother started talking fast. At first, she said, she received the message incorrectly and thought that I was in danger. Then, *they* said no, no, no, she'd had it all wrong. *They* were confusing her, the voices were all mumbled, she said, and she kept talking faster and faster.

I felt the room start to spin as if I were in the eye of a tornado, and I just wanted it all to stop. I wanted my mom to stop talking, I wanted my dad to walk down the stairs. I didn't know why, but I wanted to be living in my grandmother's basement again. I wanted to be far, far, away from home, and I wanted the goddamn light to appear at the top of the church. I wanted to tell her it was going to be all right, that everything was a bad dream. She kept saying *they, they, they, they* . . .

"Who the hell are *they*?" I finally yelled this at her, and she seemed to snap out of whatever it was she was going through. Her body relaxed as if some spell had been broken and she looked me in the eyes, her head tilted to the side.

"God, Jesus, and Mary," she said.

"What?"

"And they won't do anything to stop it."

"Mom, it's just a nightmare."

"Go to bed," she said.

I said nothing but turned and walked upstairs. My room was right above the room my mother was in, so I went to the window and pulled back the curtain. I looked outside at the cathedral, shrouded in shadow, looking like some ominous blind monster waiting to pounce on me. I felt bad for my mom and wanted to go back downstairs, but soon I heard her footsteps rise up the stairs and a door close. I looked back outside and tried to remember if I had ever seen the steeple black like that before. I couldn't think of an instance ever, but then again I didn't always look outside at night, so how would I have known?

I got into bed and tried to sleep, but I kept thinking about what had just happened, my mom's face and her words, which rolled over in my mind like a toy falling down a flight of stairs. I felt dizzy, but after awhile I came to believe that my mother had simply had a bad dream. Eventually sleep overtook me.

ON MARCH 20, 1983, a week after the incident with my mother, I was sitting in the living room watching the evening news on television. It was a Sunday, a week before Palm Sunday and two weeks before Easter, and my family and I had spent the morning spring-cleaning in our backyard. It had been a quiet day, a weekend like plenty of other weekends. Everyone was getting along and my parents had taken me to a comic-book store I loved in nearby Levittown. We had eaten dinner around four o'clock as we normally did on weekends, and my mom and sisters were in the kitchen cleaning dishes.

The breaking story was about the murder of a fourteen-year-old boy from Long Island. Since all the major stations at the time—ABC, CBS, and NBC—were based out of New York City, Long Island hardly ever received mention on the evening news (the Amy Fisher incident was still years away), so I paid close attention. Besides, I was only thirteen at the time and it was startling to hear that a boy so close to my own age had been killed. As the newscaster continued, the story grew even more unsettling.

The murder had taken place in our town, Rockville Centre. The victim had been stabbed several times and left in an alley near an old abandoned gas station on Merrick Road. A brief picture of the area, roped off by police, flashed on the screen. I knew that place! My father and I had driven past there for years. It was right across the street from the hospital where my youngest sister, Annie, had been born two years earlier.

The newscaster continued, revealing the name of the boy, Christopher Grun. I replayed all the names I knew from school and around town, and thankfully I didn't know a Christopher Grun. I did know a Christopher Gruhn, an eighth-grader at St. Agnes. He was a friend from school, and had taught me how to make toilet-paper balls and then throw them against the ceiling in the boy's lavatory. He was also the brother of a girl in my grade. But that couldn't have been the same person, could it? The newscaster pronounced the name Grun like "run," not Gruhn, like "broom."

I turned away from the TV and saw my mother standing in the doorway of the kitchen, her face drawn of all its blood as she started to cry. A few moments later, the phone rang and my mother and I stared at each other. Time seemed to stop, each ring lasting an eternity, the silence in between even longer. Finally, my mother picked up the receiver. It was one of the mothers from St. Agnes.

The newscaster had mispronounced the name.

Chapter 3

In June 2007, Grace called me at work to tell me she was pregnant. This was great news. She was happy, as was I, but she spoke in calm, cautious tones, much differently than she had earlier in the year when, out of excitement, she almost accidentally stabbed me in the eye with her First Response home pregnancy test. The last few months had been a great struggle for her both mentally and physically. She was sad and tired all the time and she kept replaying the scene in the doctor's office when she first heard the news about the miscarriage. She questioned everything about the time leading up to that moment—the foods she ate, the exercises she did, the vitamins she took, the thoughts she was thinking—hoping to find some explanation about why it had happened. She was "twisted up in knots" and just "felt off," she would tell me.

And she had trouble sleeping. So did I.

BAKHTAK IS not only the Persian word for "nightmare," it is also a demon who sits on a sleeping person's chest with the intent to suffocate. In English folklore the evil spirit is known as the Old Hag, its name derived from a medieval belief that witches would ride unsuspecting victims at night, drawing away the breath and crushing the lungs. Sufferers of such attacks recount the sounds of footsteps entering a room when no one was present, abhorrent smells, or the sight of a ghastly, revolting creature crawling upon their bodies. Today, science refers to it as sleep paralysis, a medical condition where a person's brain awakes from a cycle of REM sleep, but the body's nervous system remains at rest, leading to panic and hallucinations. While most doctors believe that it can be caused by lack of sleep or stress, many outside the medical community believe it is a form of psychic attack from a malevolent force.

On and off while growing up I had a recurring dream where I would see a figure with really big, black eyes standing over my bed. He was the color of shadow and wouldn't move until he realized I saw him. Then he would walk over, grab me by the throat, and start to choke me. I would fight back, but it would be no use. He would push me down into the bed, and I would feel pressure on my chest as if he had placed con-crete blocks on me. The dream never lasted long, but it was terrifying. When I woke up, I would be shaking and gasping for breath. I hadn't had dreams like that since I was a teen-ager, but recently they had started up again.

Late one night, I had switched places with Eddie, who was also having trouble sleeping. He went with Grace in our bed, and I took his. The strange electric surge in his room had waned a bit. I would still feel it from time to time but not like I had in the spring. I assumed that I had been correct in my initial assumption that whatever it was had to do with the weather and the temperatures inside and outside the house. (Granted, my son's electric toys—his trucks, his trains, his talking animals—would spontaneously fire off on an almost regular basis. Grace noticed this also, but we continued to chalk it up to bad batteries.) I fell asleep with the door to the room open. At some point I awoke, or at least I thought I did. I was lying on my back and I turned my head and saw the bathroom light was on. Then, something dark moved across the hallway and stood in the doorway. It looked like the shadow of a person. It had no face. It had no hands. It didn't move. My heart started to race. I tried to jump out of the bed, but I couldn't move. I felt like my chest was being crushed and the more I moved the more my rib cage felt like it was going to explode. I panicked. I gasped for air. I felt like I did when I was fourteen and challenged my cousin to swim across a small lake and almost drowned, the brown muddy water surrounding me and filling my lungs and dragging me down, saved only by some strange burst of strength and clarity. I tried again to lift myself up, but to no avail. I didn't know what to do.

At some point, I realized I was dreaming. It had to be a dream. I just wanted to wake up and tried willing myself to snap out of it even as I felt myself being pressed deeper and deeper into the bed. I felt like I was being buried alive. I struggled and tried to move my hands but nothing. I could feel my torso contorting as I tried to lift myself up and felt like I was being wrapped up in a sheet. I freaked and called out to God to help me, and it was then that I woke up, and not just woke up, but woke up to the sound of my son's toy racetrack car revving on the floor.

I lay there panting, petrified. There was no figure in the room, no shadow, just the almost metallic sound of a child's plaything. I was sweating and thought for a moment that I was still dreaming. But this part wasn't a dream. I listened to the whirling and wanted it to stop, but I was afraid to get out of the bed. In a few moments though, fear turned to frustration and impatience turned to anger and I yelled out, "Cut the shit."

The toy stopped and I lay there in silence. After a few moments, I sat up in bed, looked around, and could still feel my heart pounding in my ears. In recent months, I had taken

up reciting the Jesus Prayer, a simple seven-word mantra—
Lord Jesus Christ have mercy on me—that I would repeat throughout the day. It was a simple way of filling the seconds and
minutes of daily life with God and I would repeat it, for example, when I was walking to work, stopped at a red light, or
waiting on the checkout line at the supermarket as the ca-
shiers changed shifts (which happens to me every single
time). Instead of focusing on the impatience I might be feeling during those in-between times when I was moving from
one place to another, I would shift my focus to the Divine. I
had first heard about this prayer years ago when I was reading
J. D. Salinger's *Franny and Zooey*, but in the last few months I had
been reading the original text it was drawn from, *The Way of
the Pilgrim*, written by an anonymous nineteenth-century Russian monk.

I must have recited it a hundred times before I got out
of bed, walked to the hallway, and peeked in on Grace and
Eddie, who were sleeping soundly. I went to the bathroom,
and as I turned around to leave, I thought I saw a shadow out
of the corner of my eye and then the laundry basket, which
was sitting up against the hamper, moved ever so slightly. I
stood for a moment, looked around the room, and took a
deep breath. I shook my head, and decided I needed to start
using that prayer before I went to sleep every night. I turned
off the bathroom light, walked back to the room, got into
bed, and eventually fell asleep.

. . .

LES HALLES IS A RAMBUNCTIOUS, loud, and fast-paced French restaurant located on Park Avenue South, a couple blocks east of New York's Madison Square Park. With its dark wood interior, porcelain white tablecloths, dim gas-lamp-like lighting, attractive maître d's, no-nonsense waitstaff, and delicious onion soup (one of the best I've ever tasted), it is a culinary landmark in the legendary Flatiron District of the city, a famous restaurant made even more famous in recent years by bad-boy chef and author Anthony Bourdain. It is also one of my favorite places in the world.

In late summer 2007, I was at Les Halles having lunch with my friend Peggy, a publishing colleague and someone I'd known and trusted for some time. It had been months since I'd last seen her, and we had a lot to catch up on. We talked about work and gossiped about the publishing business, about who was doing what to whom and what the big books were for the fall. She had asked about married life and about my son. I told her Grace was pregnant but I didn't mention the miscarriage, which we had pretty much kept to ourselves. Then, I don't know why I brought it up, and I didn't go into great detail at all, but I mentioned to her briefly the strange occurrences that were happening in my house—the feelings of being watched, the bad dreams, and the odd sensations I was experiencing. I still hadn't told Grace about all this weirdness. Even though I would occasionally feel unsettled by some of the experiences, I was ultimately convinced that it was just my imagination playing tricks on me, that it was some form of cognitive dissonance where my brain was building bridges and connecting unrelated events, albeit sometimes in a very frightening way. "Nonsense linking sense," I would tell myself. But it felt good to tell another person, and after my half-minute confession, Peggy's eyes widened and she said, almost gleefully, "You have a ghost in your house."

"No, I don't," I half replied, half laughed.

"You do, you do. Those are telltale signs of genuine ghost activity."

Peggy and I had never talked like this before. Our conversations in the past had always been pleasant and interesting and ranged from politics to religion to great books we loved to read. But we never ventured into this type of territory. I shook my head and playfully told her I didn't believe her, but my curiosity was piqued and I asked her how she was so certain.

She told me about an upcoming book that was publishing in the fall called *When Ghosts Speak* by Mary Ann Winkowski, who was the real-life inspiration for the TV drama *Ghost Whisperer*. Mary Ann could see and speak to ghosts or, as she called them, earthbound spirits, the souls of the departed that had, for one reason or another, not crossed over to the other side.

I listened to Peggy as she told me more about this woman and how Mary Ann could tell if you had a ghost in your house by just talking to you on the phone.

"Wait, she can do this over the phone?" I interrupted.

"Yes," she said, "she comes to people's houses to clean them of ghosts, but she lives in Cleveland and can do what she does over the phone for people out of state. I don't know how she does it, but she does it and she's amazingly accurate."

"So she's like a psychic?" I was mildly intrigued. Though I didn't say this out loud, I had always wanted to talk to a psychic, more as an experiment than to see what my future was. Some years before, I had read a book on *cold reading*, a way of asking general questions that leads a person to think that you know more than you do, and I was curious to see if a psychic would use those techniques. But something freaked me out about them and while I would never pass judgment, I was trying really hard to be a good Catholic at the time, and as far as I knew psychics were taboo and off-limits.

"Don't call her a psychic!" Peggy laughed. "She's very particular about what she does. She talks to earthbound spirits and that's it."

Peggy, who had spoken to Mary Ann on the phone once before concerning the marketing for her book, called her the real deal and asked if I would be interested in talking to her. I said I would be, but after the words left my mouth I wished I could have taken them back. I don't know why, but something just made me nervous about the whole thing. Peggy must have sensed my apprehension because she said, "Mary Ann is one of the nicest people I've ever talked to. You would never think she was someone who could speak to ghosts. I'll get you her number and you should call her." She told me Mary Ann had a waiting list, but I should leave her a message and as soon as she could she would get back to me.

Our food arrived and shortly thereafter the conversation switched back to the publishing industry. After lunch Peggy reassured me that she would get me Mary Ann's number. I smiled but this time didn't answer, and we hugged and said good-bye.

As I walked back to work, I went over Peggy's words in my head. I started thinking about everything that had happened over the last few months and how uneasy I had been about all of it. Was it all just coincidences stacked upon coincidences? Was it stress? Could I really have a ghost in my house? And if I did, what did that mean? How could I get rid of it? I thought about my mom and some of the things she had said over the years about the ghost woman who lived in our house. I thought about the night the church light went out. I thought about the creaks and whispers and the times the doorbell would ring in the middle of the night when I was a kid and how no one was ever there and how it terrified me. Was it just pranks, or had something been trying to scare us or get our attention? I felt myself drawing connections between events that I was sure were not related in any way. Or were they? Grace had fallen down the stairs earlier in the year and felt like something had been behind her when she fell. Did she just slip or did something push her? I was constantly losing my keys and wallet—was I just being absentminded or had something hidden them? Lightbulbs were constantly going out, and the closet door downstairs in the dining room always seemed to be opened when we walked back into a room. Bad lamps and senior moments? All of a sudden, I wasn't so sure.

As I neared my office building on Twenty-sixth Street, I caught hold of my mind and gave it a shake. *Relax. It's all in your imagination,* I thought. And silly as it may seem, the *Scooby-Doo* catchphrases started running through my head: "There're no such things as ghosts" and "There's always a logical explanation for everything."

Still, I felt like I wanted to go to church, to sit and pray and talk to God about all this, but there were no churches nearby, so when I got back to my office, I closed the door, made the sign of the cross, shut my eyes, and started to quietly pray.

THE CLOUD OF UNKNOWING is a fourteenth-century text written by an anonymous English Catholic mystic. In it, the author attempts to demonstrate how one can find God in the fog of any situation, whether it be something joyful or disturbing. One way he suggests doing this is to find a quiet place and choose a word, like *hope* or *love* and repeat it to yourself, allowing your body and mind to be drawn closer to God, who is ever present inside you. Essentially, it's a mantra, like the Jesus Prayer, and the more you repeat it to yourself the closer you move toward an awareness of God. All prayer, essentially, is a chiropractic tool for the soul, a way of popping things into alignment.

I was feeling out of whack, so as I sat in my office I began to repeat the word *answer* over and over in my head. All I wanted was an answer from God. What was going on in my house? While I wasn't convinced that it was anything supernatural, I still felt a certain uneasiness about it all. Maybe I was nervous about becoming a father again or I was overtired from getting up early every day to pray and do research. So I repeated the word over and over and over again, and within a few minutes I felt a great peace move over me. I hadn't received any answer while I was praying, but as I found out over the last ten years, answers almost never come during prayer. For me, they always came afterward, and as I opened my door and resumed work, I was certain that the answer would eventually reveal itself.

For the rest of the afternoon, I answered e-mails, reviewed a couple of submissions, and wrote some copy, then went home. I was feeling better than I had after lunch and, though I still didn't have my answer and I still wasn't sure how I felt about the circus of thoughts that had gone through my head earlier in the day, I tried to forget about everything as best I could.

I didn't hear from Peggy again until a couple of weeks later. She gave me the number. I wrote it down and put it in my wallet and, while I was still uncertain about what had been going on over the last few months, I was sure about one thing.

There was no way in hell I was going to make that phone call.

SHORTLY AFTER MY MEETING with Peggy, the electric surges over my body returned in full force and I began to see unexplained shadows out of the corners of my eyes on a regular basis. I tried to ignore these things as much as possible. My uncertainty had turned into annoyance, and instead of feeling fear I was finding it a bit comical. If I was in Eddie's room with him or Grace or the two of them together, I felt nothing. If I was in there alone, then I felt like Yogi Bear covered in a huge glob of honey being attacked by a swarm of flies. At times I would stand outside the room and place one foot inside, as if I were dipping a toe into a cold stream, just to see if I would feel anything in my leg. I never did.

One night in late August, Grace and I were giving Eddie

a bath. I ran into his room to get another washcloth and as I crossed over the threshold I expected something to happen. But nothing did. It was the first time in weeks that I didn't feel the surge move up and down my spine. I actually stood there in the middle of the room for a few seconds waiting for it until Grace called out and asked what was taking me so long. I left the room, traded places with her, and started washing Eddie's hair with the washcloth. I finished the bath, wrapped him in a towel, and carried him through the hallway to his room.

As we neared his door, Eddie started to squirm in my arms so much that I had to put him down. He slid from my hands and with wet feet he nearly slipped on the floor. I bent down to pick him up and he screamed that he didn't want to go into his room. I couldn't get a hold of him. He flopped around like a fish, then his body tightened. He arched his back and neck and he felt like he weighed a hundred pounds. I grabbed him by the arms and I could feel him slipping out of my hands. I was afraid I was going to drop him. I lowered him to the floor and yelled, "You're going to hurt yourself!" He pushed me and repeated that he didn't want to go into his room and he broke away from me and ran into Grace, wrapping himself around her legs as she walked out of our bedroom. She picked him up.

"What's wrong?" she asked.

I didn't know how to answer. Eddie was shaking in her arms and I didn't know if it was because he'd just come out of the bath or something else. I walked into his room and felt the electricity crawl all over me. I tried to shake it off as I walked across the room. I turned off the light, stood in the darkness for a moment, and looked around, half expecting something to jump out of the corner or grab my leg from under the bed. Nothing happened. I walked back across the room and closed the door. Grace was standing in the hallway hugging Eddie, who had wrapped himself around her like a blanket.

"Eddie is going to sleep with us tonight," I said.

"Oh my God," Grace said. There was fear in her face.

"What?"

"Is there a mouse in the room?"

"No, it's not a mouse."

"Is it a rat? I've been hearing strange things in the attic."

"Nope, not a rat."

"Then what is it?"

"Grace, there's something we should talk about."

Chapter 4

After we put Eddie to sleep in our room, Grace and I went downstairs and sat by the picture window. I looked out and could see the light on the church steeple and the iron cross above it. I told her everything that had been happening to me over the last few months: the strange sensations in Eddie's room, the odd shadows, the frightening dreams, the toys coming to life in the middle of the night. I told her about my conversation with Peggy. I admitted it all sounded insane, that I was probably just drawing connections between totally unrelated incidents, but that it was strange nonetheless. And now with Eddie's outburst . . .

She sat quietly and patiently as I rambled on, but as I continued talking I watched her face tighten and her eyes narrow. When I was done, we just sat there in silence. I thought, "Well, this is it, she's thinks I'm crazy. She's going to take Eddie and I'll never see them again."

Grace shook her head and looked me in the eyes. "Strange things have been happening to me, too."

She went on to tell me how she had felt like she was being watched when she was home with Eddie during the day. Not by someone outside the house, but by someone inside the house. But there was never anybody there. She heard sounds on the stairs and others in the attic, but wrote it off as nothing. The house, she said, always made noise. It just happened to be louder than usual. And she had seen dark shadows out of the corners of her eyes too, but thought they were just floaters crossing her field of vision. Though, she had to admit, there was one incident that startled her a few weeks ago.

There is a small room adjacent to the kitchen with a washer and dryer and a door that leads to the backyard. It serves as a temporary dumping ground for anything that might need to be put away in the attic, in closets, or on shelves, kind of a purgatory for household items. It's not uncommon to find books, sports equipment, or toys stacked in piles waiting to be returned to their proper home. Except for near the stairs, we had stopped using safety gates after Eddie turned three. Even though we didn't block the way, Eddie knew that the washroom was off-limits. Occasionally, however, he would peek in there and see something that stirred his interest, like a dirty sock or a box that needed to be recycled.

One afternoon, Grace was washing dishes in the kitchen while our son played with his toys in the living room. The TV set was on low, and at some point she heard Eddie move behind her. Turning, she saw him dart into the washroom. Annoyed, she turned off the sink and, with wet hands, went after him, afraid that he would get hurt. When she walked into the room, he wasn't there. She looked around, walked back into the kitchen, and stepped into the living room. There was Eddie on the floor playing quietly with a dinosaur as if he had been there all day. She was sure she had seen something but wrote it off as just her eyes playing tricks on her.

There had been other instances, too. A few days after that time in the kitchen, she was in the bathroom putting away towels when she saw something move near the shower curtain. She walked over, thinking it was a big moth, pulled the curtain to the side, but saw nothing. On other occasions she noticed that one of Eddie's stuffed animals had started talking on its own, but as with the Kermit the Frog doll incident, she didn't give it much thought. She said none of this frightened her, though she had thought it was all odd. And like me, she said nothing. They all seemed like nonevents.

She asked me if I thought it was all related and I said I didn't know.

"Maybe it's my dad," she said.

Since he had passed away, Grace believed her father had become her guardian angel. From time to time she felt his presence and could smell the cigarettes he smoked when he was alive. She admitted that millions of people smoked Parliaments, but what was strange was that she often experienced the smell in our house, where none of us smoked. Grace didn't believe in ghosts. She did, however, believe in her father, whom she trusted more than anyone in her life. She knew that he would protect her and her family whether in this life or in the afterlife.

But she quickly discarded what she said. Whatever she had felt didn't feel like her dad. In fact, she said, it hadn't felt like anything at all.

I brought up what just happened with Eddie after his bath, about how he refused to go into his room and asked if she didn't think it was odd.

"That's what three-year-olds do. They don't want to sleep by themselves. I don't blame them," she said. "The dark can be scary for a little kid."

She looked at me, expecting a reply, but I didn't say anything. After a few moments she answered my silence by saying, "It's nothing. I think it's all just a coincidence. It's been a stressful time. Think of all the times non-weird stuff happens. That's most of our lives. I think you're just reading into things."

I thought about what she said and quickly replayed the

events of the last several months in my mind. I tried to convince myself that she was right, that I was making something out of nothing. Maybe it was all just coincidence. But since I had started researching Saint Ignatius—and other great Christian mystics—I had begun to believe, as they did, that everything was connected to everything else. For a long time, I had understood this intellectually. Though I was no scientist, it made the most sense to me when I would think of the big bang theory.

It was Georges Lemaître, a Belgian Catholic priest, who in 1931 first proposed before the British Science Association the theory that the creation of the universe began with a tremendous cosmological event, an explosion that originated from a dense hot spot. This "exploding cosmic egg," as he called it, essentially spewed matter into the universe, effectively leading to the development of stars, suns, moons, planets, animals, and people. If all things originated from one point, that means that all things today can trace their ancestry back to that single moment. That meant that physically we were made of stars and stars were made of us and that regardless of where we, as humans, came from—whether it be Africa or Mexico—or who our parents were, we all had the same blood running through our bodies, whether I was O negative and another person was A positive.

Now something was stirring inside me, and I began to move past believing in the almost clichéd idea that we are all connected in a physical sense to seeing it for the first time in a spiritual context. Though it was still unclear to me exactly what that was, I could feel something bubbling within. Maybe I was reading into things, as Grace said. Or maybe, just maybe, God was trying to tell me something.

All of this began to move around inside my head as I sat there with Grace until I finally said to her, "You're probably right, but what if we are *supposed* to read into things?"

PART II

Discernment of Spirits

There are two truths which people today have almost
completely forgotten. The first is that man is a fallen
creature, which means that he once possessed certain
spiritual powers that can now only be present in him
in weakened state; they can thus only become
effective under certain exceptional conditions, and
even then only in an imperfect way. The second truth
is that, although it is connected with the body, the
soul is a spirit which may sometimes loosen that
connection and may thus be able to achieve things
that would ordinarily be impossible.

—Father Alois Weisinger

Chapter 5

In September 2007, I enrolled in the Pastoral Formation Institute (PFI) through the Diocese of Rockville Centre. PFI was a three-year program designed for Catholic laypeople as a means of seeking out a vocation within the Church and offered studies in the Bible, Christian spirituality, Church history, and human sexuality, to name just a few. For years, I had been thinking about becoming a deacon, a minister who assists priests in preaching and administering the sacraments. I had prayed and discerned about it for a long time, but I still wasn't sure if it was a good fit for my personality. A deacon's job was to be at the disposal of the bishop—an honorable job, but one that I felt I might have a teeny, tiny problem with since I had always had a problem with authority figures.

Nonetheless, after talking to a couple of priest friends and speaking with a spiritual adviser, I decided that this program might do me some good and lend some structure to my religious pursuits.

That fall was a busy time. The publishing industry always went a little crazy in the months leading up to Christmas, and this year was no exception. Grace was in her second trimester and nervous about her pregnancy after what had happened earlier in the year. Eddie, who was about to turn four, was still a rambunctious and growing little boy, a three-and-a-half-foot nucleus with a never-ending supply of energy. Add to that mix school, which I attended in the evenings, and the book I was researching and writing and there was little time left for anything else.

Yet after my conversation with Grace about the unexplained things happening in our house, I found myself in need of answers, not necessarily about the incidents themselves (although that was part of it), but what all of this meant to me spiritually. Since God created all things, then all things had a spiritual component no matter how great or how small. Grace was convinced that it was all nothing—and she may have been right—but the fact that she had been experiencing similar incidents within the same time frame was enough to tip the scales for me. I kept thinking about what Peggy had said about our house having a ghost. In the back of my mind, I think I always thought so too but had been afraid to articulate it. Almost overnight I found myself filled with questions as if I were a little kid. Were ghosts and spirits real and, if so, what did my faith have to say about it? Did Catholicism even include a belief in ghosts? I was pretty sure it didn't, but I didn't really know.

In all my years, in all my reading, in all the spiritual retreats I had attended, I had never heard of someone even mentioning the word *ghost* except as an archaic term for the Holy Spirit. If the Church did believe ghosts existed, why were these things rarely discussed? And if there really was a ghost in the house, was it a good ghost or bad ghost? Was it an angel or was it a devil? What was a demon? The Bible talked about people being possessed by demons, but I always thought it was just an ancient people's misdiagnosis of epilepsy or some kind of multiple personality disorder. What did demons look like? What did they do? I had heard of exorcisms and, like most people, had seen and been frightened by the movie *The Exorcist*. I had even read a book for work written by Malachi Martin called *Hostage to the Devil*. It was published in the 1970s and was supposed to be a nonfiction account of twentieth-century exorcisms, but it seemed more fiction than fact. Was any of this real? Could a ghost be a demon or a devil?

I had made friends with a few people in PFI who never talked about ghosts but talked about the "enemy," the devil, in real terms, as if he were a living person. They had said the closer you get to God, the more the devil will try to tempt you. Was my research for a book on prayer attracting some demonic force in an attempt to derail me from the project? All these questions sounded so superstitious and so medieval to me that I could see why the Church might keep a tight lid on such things. It was more than easy, with a little imagination, to get carried away by frightening thoughts and images and lose sight of God.

My curiosity, however, had been piqued, to say the least. I didn't know if I was about to walk down the same snooping path that killed the cat, but there was something bubbling in me and I needed to figure it out. I realized that in the last six months, except for that one time in my office after my lunch with Peggy, I had not prayed about any of this since it started happening. So I did just that, I prayed, but I also discerned.

DISCERNMENT IS A FANCY WORD for a decision-making process, and one most favored by Saint Ignatius. In a nutshell, a person enters into spiritual discernment when he or she has come to some sort of crossroads. Should I take this new job or stay where I am? Should I get married or stay single? Should I help someone who has repeatedly let me down or not? You propose the question to God, you pray, and then you listen. Sometimes the listening takes a long time, sometimes not. If an answer comes and it brings peace, then it's the right thing to do. If not, keep on praying.

Saint Ignatius also believed that when you enter into discernment you need to be aware of what it is you're resisting in your life. If, for example, someone has mistreated you and you hold a grudge and are unable to forgive that person, Ignatius would want you to become very conscious of where the resistance is coming from. Is it a bruised ego? Is it out of fear? Is it out of a need for revenge? Whatever it is, it's a signal that something is out of alignment and you need prayer, guidance, and assistance to help you arrive at a place where there is no resistance, just forgiveness. Essentially, one key that unlocks the door leading to spiritual growth can be found in that which you reject. (This, of course, presupposes that what you're rejecting is contrary to the golden rule— love God and love your neighbor as yourself. If someone tells you to kill another person and you resist, well, that's a good thing because you're not supposed to kill anyone. Duh.)

For months I had been resisting my gut feeling that whatever I was experiencing was something supernatural. I thought back to how I dug in my heels when Peggy suggested there might be a ghost in my house and then again when Grace suggested there wasn't. Why was I resisting both belief and nonbelief?

I must admit that both ideas in some ways frightened me. I had tried to ignore a number of feelings over the last few months, but now I wanted to take action. But what to do? I had no idea, really. I wasn't ready to call the number Peggy had given me and I wasn't ready to talk to anyone else about this either. So I put the matter before God. I prayed and asked what I should do.

And I didn't get an answer.

I prayed on it for a week and nothing. Activity was still happening in the house. I continued to see shadows out of the corners of my eyes. Ed's toys continued to talk on their own. I had no idea that he had so many cars and stuffed animals that made noise. We changed the batteries on some and it still kept happening. And then one night, while Grace and I were watching TV, we heard what sounded like a window breaking right in the middle of the room, as if someone were standing in front of us with a pane of glass and whacked it with a hammer. Grace was startled. I jumped up off the couch and ran outside, thinking that someone had tried to break one of our windows, but there was no one around. I searched all around the house, inside, outside, and found nothing. No broken glass. It wasn't until the next day that I remembered this used to go on in our house when I was a kid. Sometimes my dad thought I was responsible since I had a tendency to throw baseballs around the house (I know, I was an idiot), but after inspecting everything he never found even the smallest sliver of glass anywhere.

At this point I had had enough and even though the process of discernment seemingly hadn't worked for me, I had made a decision to finally do something. I wish I could say it was something dramatic, but the first thing I did is what most nerdy people in publishing do when they want an answer: read.

Having worked with books for over ten years, I had seen peripherally a number of them that engaged the whole ghost debate—were spirits and phantoms real or just stories meant to scare schoolchildren? On one side were the rationalists, who believed in a very modern view that all that's real in the world is that which can be seen and touched and examined by science. If science couldn't prove it, or at least give a pretty decent, logical theory, then it was nonsense. Then there were the believers, who were adamant that there was a spirit world regardless of the lack of physical evidence or the mostly inaccurate predictions, or obvious observations, of mediums or psychics. While I would eventually make my way to both types of books and arguments over the course of several months, I was most interested in knowing what the Catholic Church had to say about all this, if they had anything to say at all. So I started with the place I have visited a number of times over the years when I was looking for answers to questions of faith. No, not the Bible, but John Hardon.

John Hardon was a Jesuit priest who had studied philosophy at Loyola University and theology at the Gregorian University in Rome. He taught for some years at St. John's University in Queens. He was a brilliant, devout, faithful, and levelheaded man who wrote a number of intelligent but accessible works on Catholic theology, including *The Catholic Catechism* in 1975,* which was the first time a book brought together the teachings of the Church in one single volume. He was also the author of the *Modern Catholic Dictionary*. Those two books had taught me more about the foundations of my faith than any other, and Hardon had become my go-to author whenever I needed information. Though he wasn't the official spokesperson for the Catholic Church, he was pretty darn close. If there were any Church teachings on ghosts, Hardon would know about it.

By this time it was early October and Eddie had become a permanent fixture in our bed. Grace, who still didn't believe that anything weird was going on, had tried on a couple of occasions to have him return to his room. But he was adamant about not going back. Grace was growing more and more tired as her pregnancy progressed and refused to press the issue. This was fine by me. I had come to believe that there was *something* in the house and that Eddie's room was a hot spot of sorts, so I didn't object. Still, I found myself vacillating between belief and nonbelief. Though I had made the agreement with myself to start my own personal investigation into the supernatural, it was another week before I made any attempt to see what Hardon might know about ghosts.

---

*It has since been surpassed by the official *Catechism of the Catholic Church*, released by the Vatican in 1992. John Hardon served as a consultant on that version. His books, however, are still well respected and sought out today for their literary quality.

On a warm, windy night after Grace and Eddie were asleep I rolled out of bed and made my way to the attic, where the bulk of my books were. I tried to be as quiet as possible, but every step I took seemed to echo throughout the hall. The attic, like the basement, had never been my favorite part of the house, probably because its low ceiling and exposed walls made me feel claustrophobic. I opened the door, closed it behind me, and walked up the stairs. I moved some boxes of summer clothes that Grace had recently put up there and started searching the bookshelf that held my books on the Catholic Church. I found Hardon's dictionary pretty quickly.

As I took the book down, a burst of doubt went off in my head. Just about anything that was of any importance to the Catholic Church could be found in this book—from the definition of *ad majorem Dei gloriam* (for the greater glory of God) to the explanation of who Zephaniah was (author of the ninth book of the minor prophets)—and I was certain at that moment that none of what had been going on inside my head was important. I sat on the floor and as I began flipping through the pages I was pretty sure that there would be no entry for *ghost*.

I heard something moving downstairs and stopped to listen, but it quickly went away. I thought that I might have been too loud moving boxes and stirred Grace or Eddie from sleep. I waited a few moments and when I didn't hear anything else, I turned to the *Gs* and started running my finger down the page and, just as I suspected, there was no entry. I felt a mixture of relief and disappointment and wasn't sure what to do next. If Hardon had nothing to say on the subject it probably wasn't worth exploring. I closed the book and as I was about to put it away, something made me open it again. I did so, went back over the *Gs*, and I don't know how I missed it the first time, but on the bottom of page 229, was this:

Ghost. A disembodied spirit. Christianity believes that God may, and sometimes does, permit a departed soul to appear in some visible form to people on earth. Allowing for legend and illusion, there is enough authentic evidence, for example in the lives of the saints, to indicate that such apparitions occur. Their purpose may be to teach, or warn, or request some favor of the living.

"Get out," I said to myself.

Did this really mean that the Church actually believed in the existence of ghosts? Hell, if Hardon said it, that was enough for me. I quickly flipped through the book, looking up words like *phantom* and *poltergeist,* but I didn't find any of those. I did, however, find entries on angels and demons. To my surprise, it seemed that the Church didn't consider these to be literary conceits, metaphors, or remnants from a superstitious age, but living—and very powerful—presences in our world today.

At creation, God created the angels. They were unlike

humans in that they were pure intelligence and invisible with no bodies. But they did share one thing in common with mankind: free will. They had the ability to decide on whether to stay with God or break free. The angels kept with God, the ones that didn't, by their act of defiance, became demons. Both could, and did, have influence on humanity.

I kept turning the pages back and forth and found entries on telepathy and clairvoyance, the ability to read minds; levitation; bilocation, the ability to be in two places at once, a lot like the New Age and shamanistic belief of astral projection; stigmata, experiencing the physical wounds of Jesus. The Church didn't deny the existence of any of these things, but saw them as very real occurrences. Sometimes they were signs of angelic influence and sometimes they were signs of demonic activity, discerning which was which was, it turned out, a very real gift of the Holy Spirit.

As I kept reading, my arms became covered in gooseflesh and I felt a chill run up my back. I realized how different that feeling was from what I had been experiencing in Eddie's room over the last few months. I kept scanning the pages—there were entries for archangels, guardian angels, Satan, Lucifer— all the while hearing faint movements downstairs, which I tried to ignore until the door clicked open.

"Grace?" I called out.

But there was no answer.

I closed the book and made my way to the stairs. I looked

down and saw that the attic door was open a crack. I just stared at it for a few moments and then whispered Grace's name again, but there was no reply. I walked down, turned off the light, closed the door quietly, and stood still, trying to listen to the house. Had I not fully closed the door behind me? Did the wind find its way through the cracks? Something like this, a door opening on its own, had happened a few times before in our house, during a storm, but why now? Why tonight? Had something opened it?

The door to Eddie's room, which was at the foot of the stairs, was open. Inside, it was dark and quiet and I could see the sharp angles of his bed, his dresser, and toys. I looked in and I felt that something was watching me.

And in a moment of defiance, I stared right back and whispered, "I'm onto you. It may have taken me some time, but I'm onto you."

I walked back to my bedroom, where both Grace and Eddie were sound asleep. After I placed Hardon's book on the dresser, I lay in bed, going over his words in my head. *Their purpose may be to teach, or warn, or request some favor of the living.*

But which one was it?

Chapter 6

On April 2, 1839, a young Catholic seminarian named John Bosco sat in a pew in a church and mourned the death of his dear friend Louis Comollo. Six years earlier, the two had met during Bosco's last year in secondary school in Piedmont, a mostly mountainous province in northern Italy. They attended the seminary together in Chieri, an important textile town about eleven kilometers from Turin that had once been under the thumb of Napoleon Bonaparte in the late eighteenth century. They had an enduring friendship and the two complemented each other's dispositions. Comollo had always been quiet, frail, and devout; Bosco, on the other hand, while a sensitive and serious young man in his own right, was also funny, loving, and sociable. Bosco grew up in poverty, but from the age of nine believed he was on a mission from God. He had his first prophetic dream at that age when a vision, possibly of Jesus, told him that it was with charity and gentleness that he must bring people together. The dreams would continue for the rest of his life.

Though devoted to God, he was not without his doubts, and the death of his friend was a painful blow to the young student, whose father had died when he was two years old. While they were attending school together, both Bosco and Comollo were captivated by the lives of the saints and one day they made a pact. After reading about the exploits of the likes of Saint John the prophet, Saint Francis the servant, and Saint Anthony the desert hermit tormented by demons, they agreed that whoever was the first to die would bring back word of life on the other side to the surviving friend. Certainly, at the time they thought they had years before either of them would die, or did they?

That agreement resounded in Bosco's ears like the church bells that rang through the town that morning. He sat in the church and looked around for a sign from his friend— a light, a vision, a sudden movement, anything. He listened intently to the words of the funeral rite and to the sounds around him. Nothing. But Bosco was patient and vowed to keep vigil of the agreement. The words of an old dream surely passed through his mind: "What seems so impossible you must achieve by being obedient." He would be obedient and patient. He would wait as long as he had to for a sign.

Bosco didn't have to wait long. The next night, he was in his dormitory, a large open room that housed twenty other seminarians, preparing to go to sleep. It had been a long couple of days and the death of Louis Comollo was still burning inside of him. He lay in his bed and as his other roommates drifted off to sleep, Bosco prayed. He was praying to hear from his friend, to have word from heaven, to confirm for him that he was on the right path and that his dreams weren't deceptions of the mind, but direct messages from the Almighty. He lay in bed and waited when a sign, which he documented in one of the many books he wrote during his lifetime, came to pass.

On the stroke of midnight, a deep rumble was heard at the end of the corridor. The rumble became deeper and louder as it drew nearer. It was like the sound of a large cart, or a railway train, or even artillery fire. I do not know how to describe the sound adequately except to say that it was such a mixture of throbbing and rather violent sounds as to leave the hearer utterly terrified and too frightened for words.

As the rumble drew nearer it made the ceiling, walls, and floor of the hallway vibrate like sheets of metal struck by the hand of some mighty giant. Yet the sound approached so that it was very difficult to pinpoint how close it was, the way one is uncertain where a locomotive is on the track from the jet of steam.

All the seminarians in the dormitory woke up, but no one spoke. I was frozen with fear. The noise came nearer and nearer and grew more frightening. It reached the dormitory; of itself the door slammed open. The roar grew louder, but there was nothing to see except a ghostly multicolored light that seemed to control the sound. Suddenly there was silence, the light intensified, and Comollo's voice was distinctly heard: "Bosco, Bosco, Bosco—I am saved."

At that moment the dormitory grew even brighter. The noise erupted again, much longer and louder than before. It was like thunder, so violent that the house seemed about to collapse; then suddenly it stopped and the light vanished.

Bosco, who would go on to found the Society of St. Francis de Sales in 1859, and eventually be canonized a saint in 1934, had received his answer.

I had never heard a story like that when I was going to Catholic school. If I had, I would have paid better attention. And I certainly wasn't hearing stories like that in my theology classes in the fall of 2007, but a friend of mine loaned me her book on saints, so I, like John Bosco, began reading the lives of the saints on my own. While I had made no pact with my pal about one of us returning to give word of heaven, I was overwhelmed by these stories of faith, love, and charity. A whole new world of Catholicism opened before me. Here were thousands of saints from all walks of life and all parts of the world who had lived extraordinary lives of devotion, and while I was aware of this in an ancillary way, I had never much thought about them. Sure, there were statues of Saint Francis, Saint Jude, and Saint Joseph in our house growing up and in our house now, but I could never tell you more about them than one liked furry woodland creatures, one helped out when it came to lost causes, and the other was the adoptive daddy to Jesus.

But here in this book were Saint Elizabeth of Hungary, a queen who had given everything up to serve the poor; Saint Clare, who in the Middle Ages helped defend her convent and the people of Assisi from invaders; Saint Anthony, the hermit whose every breathing moment was given to prayer to God. Their stories of passion were inspiring and I felt guilty for having ignored a whole area of my faith that was so colorful and interesting. But what I found most fascinating were the supernatural events surrounding some of the saints. I had known about Francis's stigmata, that he suffered the wounds of Christ, but truth be told, I always felt that he had inflicted the wounds on himself with a couple of cigars and a medieval-style blowtorch. But I had no idea that Thérèse of Lisieux had kicked demons' asses or that Teresa of Ávila, Catherine of Siena, and even Saint Ignatius were known to levitate inches and sometimes several feet off the floor during prayer. That's pretty amazing in itself, but Saint Alphonsus Liguori one-upped them all.

In 1745, the Italian priest was preaching during Mass when a ray of light from a picture of the Blessed Virgin Mary shone down on him and raised him off the ground in front of the congregation. Twenty-nine years later he would experience bilocation, or being in two places at once, while praying. He was in his local church and all of a sudden appeared a long distance away—the equivalent of a four-day walk— sitting at the bedside of a then-dying Pope Clement XIV, assisting him into the next life. Reports of the priest's being in different places at the same time soon spread, and though there was no logical explanation, all saw it as a sign not only of his holiness, but also of the awesome power of God.

As I had found out, John Bosco had an encounter with a ghost and for most of his life experienced prophetic dreams; fourth-century John of Egypt was a clairvoyant; Saint John of the Cross, Saint Jerome, Saint Clare of Assisi, and Saint Bernadette had all experienced apparitions and saw visions of Jesus, Mary, or the future. Page after page told stories of amazing feats and daring rescues. In some ways, I felt like a kid again reading the exploits of comic-book superheroes like Superman, Batman, Wonder Woman, and Green Lantern.

Certainly, some of these stories were hagiography and legend. Or were they? Jesus had said that if you had the faith of a teeny, tiny mustard seed you could move mountains. Peter had walked on water until he became conscious of what he was doing and doubted. Doubt, in many ways, defines us in the modern world. If someone with means adopts a number of children, we don't see it as a humanitarian action, but rather as a selfish act to either have a large family or deal with some emotional scar from growing up without parents. There are relatively few public heroes in the world because the media is constantly finding ways of tearing people down. Certainly, skepticism was, and is, an important part of our world. Even doubting Thomas, who didn't believe that his friends had seen Jesus after the resurrection, was blessed with his very own encounter with Christ to prove that the miracle was real. But is what we see on TV and on blogs and in newspapers truly skepticism or just bad attitudes?

I started reviewing what I believed and realized that I had used skepticism as a mask for cynicism for most of my life. One was life-affirming, the other was life-threatening. And I was a product of my environment. Maybe the reason miracles don't seem to happen as much today as they had hundreds of years ago is that none of us can muster a fraction of an ounce of faith in ourselves or in others.

Maybe we need extraordinary things to happen to us to shake us from the sleep of doubt?

. . .

LATER THAT FALL, I began visiting old bookstores in downtown New York City searching for anything on Catholicism and the supernatural. Such books were nearly impossible to come by. These shops had plenty of books on the occult—on demonology, witchcraft, and the devil, as well as books on ghosts and the paranormal—but they were mostly New Age testimonials or practice guides. I perused some of them and felt like the proverbial fish out of water. I had spent the last ten years of my life pursuing the intellectual, philosophical, historical, and political aspect of religion in general, and Catholicism in particular, but this was new—and at times dark—terrain. This is not to say that everything I read had a sinister hue. There were interesting books on the history of alchemy and ancient folklore, as well as self-help books on how to develop your psychic skills (which I knew was a no-no in Catholicism, but didn't some of the saints possess these abilities and weren't these gifts from God?). And there were plenty of books on angels, yet again, mostly from a New Age perspective. Why weren't there more publications for Catholics?

Regardless, I was impressed that these books, especially the ones on angels, weren't forty-eight-page pamphlets, but thick tomes filled with the names and histories of spiritual beings throughout the ages. I knew of the archangels Michael and Gabriel and Raphael (the only three angels named in the Bible), but there were literally thousands and thousands of names—both angelic and demonic—that had existed and, being somewhat eternal, are still living today. Some of these were from literature like John Milton's *Paradise Lost* or Dante's *Divine Comedy*; others were from apocryphal texts like the book of Enoch or the book of Jubilees (in-between texts that fell somewhere between the writing of the Old and New Testaments). Still others were from kabbalah or gnostic testaments, while many others came from Islam, Buddhism, and the Vedic traditions known in the west as Hinduism. Again, another door to my understanding of faith was opening right before me. And angels were some serious business. These weren't the rosy-cheeked cherubs and Pre-Raphaelite angels many of us grew up seeing on posters or on greeting cards. These were some serious streetwise individuals whom you could call on in times of danger (angels and demons have no matter, but it is believed by many that they can manifest themselves to us in physical ways . . . how you do that by being pure intelligence, I have no idea). Many theologians whom I always believed were men of great faith but who were essentially men of logic believed wholeheartedly in the existence of angels—including Thomas Aquinas and Saint Augustine. Aquinas was even called the "Angelic Doctor" because his major theological treatise, the *Summa Theologica*, contained vast information about the nature of angels and is where we get most of what we know about them today.

There was Abdiel, "servant of God," the angel Milton called the "flaming seraph" who kicked the shit out of Satan on the first day of fighting in the war in heaven (this was after Satan chose not to serve God); there was Metatron, who in rabbinic tradition was one of the most powerful of the angels; and Uriel, the counselor, who asked God to spare humankind after the Almighty became fed up with the mysterious angelic Watchers who mated with beautiful women who in turn gave birth to a creation, the Nephilim, that God had never intended.

These were riveting stories and what fascinated me the most was that all this history and belief had been lost in our modern age. I'm sure I could have asked most of the people I knew and they never would have heard that there were nine angelic orders—the seraphim, cherubim, thrones, dominions, virtues, powers, principalities, archangels, and angels proper (or guardian angels). Granted, knowledge of this wouldn't get you a job or feed your kids, but wasn't it true that none of us live by bread alone?

There were also two books written by modern-day exorcists: *Interview with an Exorcist* by Jose Antonio Fortea, a Roman Catholic priest from Spain, and *An Exorcist Tells His Story* by Gabriele Amorth, a very famous priest from Rome. Both of these books demonstrated a living, breathing battle being waged in our cities and homes between the forces of good and evil.

My mind would go spinning and I would find myself losing track of time on some nights, and after purchasing a book or two I would rush to Penn Station to catch the train back to Long Island. On the ride home, I would replay in my head what I had seen and read. On many occasions I had to question whether or not I was being led on this pursuit by some strange force—I just didn't know if it was God or something else holding my hand.

Eventually, mostly by searching on the Internet, I was able to find three out-of-print books that dealt specifically with ghosts. Two were by Catholic priests: *Ghosts and Poltergeists* by Father Herbert Thurston and *Occult Phenomenon* by Father Alois Wiesinger. The third book, written by the first cousin of British prime minister Winston Churchill, who became a convert while a student at Cambridge, was titled, strangely enough, *Shane Leslie's Ghost Book*. While all three differed in tone and execution, they all agreed that ghosts were very real and very important to understand. Yet what I found most interesting as a Catholic was that each was written before the Second Vatican Council.

Though many people don't see it, the Catholic Church is constantly going through periods of reevaluating itself. No internal evaluation was more influential in recent times than the Second Vatican Council, which took place between 1962 and 1965. Though it's impossible to summarize this event in Church history succinctly, this coming together of bishops and prelates under the guidance of Pope John XXIII and later Pope Paul VI looked to bring the Church into the modern era. With destruction and loss of life from two World Wars, the growing tension between capitalism and communism, and advances in technology, to name just a few of the issues, by mid-century the Church found itself in need of new ways of approaching and dealing with the modern world. There were a number of reforms, including translating the Latin Mass into vernacular languages and the opening of lines of communication with other religions. All in all, these were radical reforms and much-needed changes that allowed the Church to minister to an ever-changing populace.

What many of the faithful thought was lost after these reforms was a sense of the supernatural—of an unseen, invisible world, the world of spirit. This is not to say that spiritual matters were abandoned. Far from it, but as the Church shifted its focus in the latter years of the twentieth century, did belief in angelic and demonic forces have a place in the modern world anymore? Did miracles really happen or could science explain them away? Or, for that matter, was heaven a real place or a state of mind? As these issues were debated over the next few decades, the idea of a spirit world for many people began to lose power. And, many critics believed, so did God.

. . .

ONE NIGHT IN EARLY DECEMBER, after Grace and Eddie fell asleep, I was downstairs reading Father Wiesinger's book on occult phenomena. At some point I fell asleep on the couch and awoke around three o'clock in the morning to see a woman with auburn hair and a floral dress standing in the doorway to Eddie's toy room. I stared at her for a moment. She didn't move but appeared to be watching me. I swallowed hard, closed my eyes, and when I opened them she was gone. I was pretty sure I was awake when I saw her, but I wasn't 100 percent sure—it could have been a strange synapse in my brain, some sort of visual image left over from a dream that I saw upon waking. Nonetheless, whether it was real or dreamt, my heart was racing and I could hear the sound of church bells. For a moment I thought they must be coming from the cathedral, so I sat up and turned my head toward the window. Then, I heard faint music mix with the bells. Having no idea what I was hearing, I got up to look out the window. The parking lot was empty, the streets silent.

The lamp was off in the toy room, which was just beyond our dining room, but there was a soft blue glow from the computer screen illuminating the wall. I stood up and slowly walked across the floor, and the church bells were replaced by the sound of drums. And it was getting louder. I stepped inside the toy room, where there was music coming out of the speakers. iTunes was on, and metallic guitars were pumping to the beat. It took me a brief moment, but the song registered in my head. It was "Hell's Bells" by AC/DC. I remembered leaving the computer on before I started reading, but I was positive there wasn't any music playing. The vocals kicked in and, as I stood there listening to the song, I felt the electric surge that I had mostly only felt in Eddie's room roll over me as lead singer Brian Johnson intoned, "I'll give you black sensations up and down your spine. If you're into evil then you're a friend of mine."

"You've got to be shitting me," I said to myself. "There is no way this is happening." I switched off iTunes, shut down the computer, walked upstairs, and got into bed with Grace. Eddie was sleeping soundly next to her. I put my arm over the both of them and, for the first time since all of this began, I felt afraid.

Chapter 7

Fall turned to winter, and the holidays came and went. I was still seeing shadows moving out of the corners of my eyes, toys continued switching on by themselves, and the strange surges continued in Eddie's room, only not as frequently. I did my best to ignore these things when they happened. If Grace had been picking up on anything, she didn't say so. And I'm pretty sure even if she had, she wouldn't have cared. She was in the last stages of her pregnancy, and the past few months had been a struggle. A sonogram a few months earlier had shown a small spot on the baby's brain. The doctors said it could be nothing or it could be something and that we should get an amniocentesis to make sure. We opted not to do that, kicking it up to God's will.

"My father will watch over the baby," Grace said. "He's his guardian angel, too."

Though we tried to be positive, little fissures of doubt nonetheless crept in, at least for me. Moreover, Grace was experiencing pain and discomfort in a way she never had when she was pregnant with Eddie. Nothing felt right and what should have been a happy time preparing for a new child was riddled with painful cramps, sometimes debilitating backaches, and severe nausea. The doctor reassured her that everything looked normal, but since she was going into the last leg before delivery, he wanted to see her at least once a week just to make sure everything was fine.

Three weeks before her due date, her symptoms seemed to dissipate. Still, a visit to the doctor was mandatory, and one afternoon I left work early so she and I could go see him together. While in the office, the nurse took her blood pressure, grimaced, shook her head, and took it again. At the end of the second time, she looked frightened, told us to wait in the room, and stepped outside. She and another nurse entered a minute later, and the new woman took the reading again. After she was done, she quickly pulled the stethoscope out of her ears, unwrapped the Velcro blood-pressure band around Grace's arm, and said matter-of-factly, "Honey, you have to go to the emergency room. Get dressed. We'll call for you now."

Grace and I looked at each other and asked what was wrong. The nurse said that Grace had the highest blood pressure she had ever seen and that there was no time to wait. She asked us if we wanted an ambulance, and I told her no, I would drive.

From her doctor's office it was a ten-minute ride to Winthrop Hospital in Mineola. Along the way, Grace looked and felt fine and we thought the nurse had been mistaken. But when we arrived at the hospital emergency room, a nurse was waiting to wheel her in. A doctor saw her immediately. She was hooked up to a monitor and quickly admitted to the maternity ward.

Grace had developed preeclampsia, a dangerous medical condition that can arise in some pregnancies. It causes high blood pressure in the mother, which in turn affects the amount of oxygen and blood the baby receives inside the womb. If undiagnosed, the disorder can turn into full-blown eclampsia, which can lead to embolisms and seizures and can be fatal for both mother and child.

She was in the hospital for a week and during that time she had daily sonograms to monitor the baby's heart rate. It was a long week, filled with uncertainty and doubt, but on February 27, her doctor decided that enough time had elapsed and the baby was far enough along to be delivered. He induced Grace, and she gave birth to Charles Jansen at 4:51 p.m. while Judge Judy ranted and raved on the TV in the background.

Charles was fine.

. . .

THAT NIGHT, after all the visitors had left, I sat with Grace and Eddie in the hospital room and stared at the new little boy who had just come into our lives. "You were a difficult little guy, weren't you?" I said to him. He didn't respond. Not that I expected him to. He was, after all, only a couple of hours old. But he was beautiful and calm and radiated peace. Wrapped in his terry-cloth hat and blanket, he looked like a tiny white bean. Grace was exhausted, and I needed to be back at work the next day, so Eddie and I left. Grace cried because she was happy and tired and was sick of being in the hospital and just wanted to go home.

I dropped Eddie off at his grandmother's. He wanted to stay with me and I wanted to stay with him. I hadn't seen him for much of the week. I had taken a number of days off from work to be with Grace while she was in the hospital and I needed to go into the office the following morning, if only for a few hours. Grace's mom had agreed to take the day off to babysit, and after I kissed Eddie good night, I drove home. It was nighttime and I could barely keep my eyes open behind the wheel. For the last week I had been terrified of losing Grace and losing the baby. Now that Charlie was here and Grace seemed to be in good shape, relief had set in. My body had been running on nerves and adrenaline, but now I was coming down—and coming down fast. I thought about getting Starbucks to wake up, but decided against it. I just wanted to close my eyes and rest.

I arrived in Rockville Centre around ten o'clock. It was the first time in a very long time that I was in the house by myself. I immediately went upstairs, kicked off my shoes, climbed into bed, and fell asleep. I didn't even change my clothes, which would have freaked Grace out if she had known. She thought hospitals were the dirtiest places in the world. I didn't disagree, but that night I just didn't care.

Around three o'clock in the morning I awoke to the sound of the doorbell ringing. I opened my eyes and didn't move. For a moment I didn't know where I was, but the sound seemed to hang in the room—as if someone had clicked a spoon against a wineglass—and then slowly faded away. My heart was pounding and I wasn't sure if I had been having a nightmare or if there was someone at the front door. My eyes darted around the room, trying to adjust to waking up. I was breathing fast and panic rose and fell in my chest. There were few things more ominous to me than the sound of a doorbell in the middle of the night and I waited to see if it would happen again. I felt like a coward, but I just couldn't bring myself to make a move. If it was just a dream, there wouldn't be a second ring, and if it was real, then whoever was there would ring again. I waited and a tiny movie played in my head of all the times our doorbell had rung in all hours of the night when I was growing up. There was never anyone there. My father always wrote it off as kids playing pranks, but if it had been a bunch of punks fooling around they never made any sound—no laughing, no collision of boys tumbling over each other to get away. And when we looked out into the street there never was anything there except streetlights and shadows.

I waited for the next bell to ring and began counting *Mississippi*s in my head the way I used to when I was a kid in between a strike of lightning and a roar of thunder to determine how far off a storm was.

One Mississippi.

Two Mississippi.

Three Mississippi.

Four . . .

Ding.

The bell rang again. The storm, which I hadn't seen coming, was standing on my doorstep.

"Goddamnit," I said and jumped out of bed, pulled back the blind, and looked out the window. No one was there, but I had a limited range of vision because the alcove below blocked the view. I jumped out of my room, ran downstairs, and swung open the door. Standing there in the darkness was nothing. I ran outside in my socks. The ground was cold and wet and I stood on the sidewalk, the streetlight shining above me like a small moon, and looked around and there was no one anywhere to be seen. The streets were empty.

"Leave us the hell alone!" I yelled out loud. And I didn't know who I was mouthing off to. Some kid, some ghost, a demon, myself? "What the hell is going on?"

I walked back inside with my heart still racing and boiled water for tea in the kitchen. The house was freezing. I warmed my hands over the stove and tried to quiet my mind. I started reciting the Jesus Prayer over and over in my head, but it didn't do much good. When the water was ready, I made the tea, then walked into the front room and adjusted the thermostat. The pipes clunked awake and the furnace blazed to life in the basement. I sat down in the dark by the picture window and looked out at the cathedral in the distance. The streetlight cast an orange glow in the room and it reminded me of the burning stub of my mother's cigarette and the night she sat in this very spot and told me of the darkness that hung over the church down the block from us. Next to me, an end table was stacked with books I was either in the process of reading or planning to read. They were mostly books on angelology and demonology. I thought maybe I needed to just throw them out and read a good Hemingway novel or dive into an issue of *Sports Illustrated*.

"Yes, strange things have been happening for the last

year, but you're probably not making it any better by reading this crap," I said out loud to myself.

Then, for the first time, I thought that we should just move, sell the house, and just go somewhere else. I had been in this place for most of my life. Why hadn't I left? I always thought it was because I felt sorry for the house and felt sorry for my parents, who tried their best to raise five kids and ended up breaking themselves in the process. I thought I felt sorry for what could have been, but maybe I didn't feel sorry for anything or anyone. Maybe the real reason I stayed was because *something was keeping me here*. I had tried to be rational about everything in recent months, but by this time I was pretty well convinced that something was in the house. And if there was, had I been irresponsible for having not done anything? Had I put my family in danger? Nothing life threatening had happened. Or had it? Had Grace's difficult pregnancy been the result of some kind of spirit, or was it just something that happened, something random?

Regardless of how strange or spooky some of the occurrences had been to me over the last year, I had no proof they were anything other than just natural events. But still something inside was telling me that there was more to the story. I knew it went beyond all logic and against everything I had believed in. Part of me still thought that maybe it was just stress, but I didn't know. I just didn't know.

In the pile of books was *When Ghosts Speak*. It was written by Mary Ann Winkowski, the woman Peggy recommended I call way back in the summer. One of our sister book clubs at work, One Spirit, had offered the book to its members in its promotional catalogs. The editor had passed along a copy to me after I had inquired about it a few weeks after my lunch with Peggy. Though my paperback division had signed on to offer the book in the summer of 2008, just on the strength of its title, I still hadn't looked at it. I put down my tea, turned on the lamp, reached over, opened the book, and read until morning. And while I was fascinated by the stories of earthbound spirits who roamed the earth for many different reasons, I was most intrigued by something else: curses.

Chapter 8

The *malocchio*, or the evil eye, is a curse inflicted on an unsuspecting individual with malevolent intent. It is the product of envy and can be done deliberately, for instance, when someone wishes another person dead, or by accident, like one friend being jealous of another friend's beauty. One casts a cold, bitter eye on another and the look can have serious repercussions. In many ways, it is akin to shooting someone with an envy bullet and is believed by many to cause headaches, misfortune, accidents, and sometimes even death.

Many believe it originated in Ancient Egypt—the eye of Horus is a symbol that protects one from its effects—and the evil eye, or a variation of it, has been documented throughout the centuries in countries as diverse as Italy, India, Bangladesh,

Pakistan, Croatia, the Dominican Republic, and Tibet. Immigrants brought the belief to the United States and though it's not often spoken about openly, many people believe in it and wear various amulets to protect themselves from it.

I first learned about the *malocchio* a month before my twenty-fifth birthday. I was excited after having bought a new car and told all my friends about it. Many people shared my enthusiasm and wished me well, even throwing dollar bills and coins on the floor of the car as a good-luck wish. I was happy to have the car and thrilled to know that in less than thirty days I would be paying lower insurance rates, since I would be moving out of the mandatory assigned risk category that all drivers under twenty-five are lumped into in New York State.

But a good buddy of mine pulled me aside one day and told me to be careful, that he knew for a fact a mutual acquaintance of ours had been jealous about the fact that I was going to be paying lower insurance premiums in less than a month. (You would think this guy would have been green-eyed because I bought a new car, but anyone under twenty-five who lives on Long Island knows all too well how much car insurance costs.) He said this person had given me the evil eye, and I asked him what that was and he told me. I laughed and told him I didn't believe in such superstitious nonsense. He understood but told me to be cautious anyway. He didn't want to see me get into an accident.

Accident?

I didn't mention what my buddy told me to anyone because I thought it was nonsense, but he said the word *accident* and you know what? He planted a tiny seed in my head like Iago did to Othello and it took root. I tried to figure out who it was that might have been talking shit about me and soon found out. I wasn't angry at the person. He was a jerk anyway, but I was furious at my buddy for having said anything to me. Now I was self-conscious and a little paranoid about crashing my car. I knew if it happened it would just be some variation of a self-fulfilling prophecy, but nonetheless, I found myself doubting myself every time I was behind the wheel. So what did I do? I drove as cautiously as I could for a month.

The morning of my birthday arrived and nothing had happened. I knew what my buddy had said about the evil eye was garbage and I felt pretty good, first for turning a quarter-century old and because I had avoided *the dreaded curse!*

My mother's car wasn't working at the time, so she asked to borrow mine. She needed to pick something up in Baldwin, a town right next to ours. I said sure. That morning, on a slick road, my mom plowed into the back of a pickup truck on Merrick Road, crumpling the front end of the car like paper. The air bag didn't deploy, and she hit her head against the steering wheel and sat there, stunned. It was an overcast day and had been drizzling, but everything looked bright to her. She felt warm and peaceful and thought for a moment that she had died and gone to heaven. Then there was a tapping at the side window. She slowly rolled it down and there was a large barrel-chested man asking her if she was all right. She looked at him and stared into his eyes. He looked familiar and it took her a moment for it to register. It was Joey Buttafuoco. Three years before, the auto body shop owner had been involved in an affair with an underage Amy Fisher, the infamous "Long Island Lolita" who put a bullet in his wife's head in a failed murder attempt.

My mom looked through the windshield at the smashed car and back to Buttafuoco and realized she hadn't died and she definitely had not gone to heaven.

My mom wasn't injured, but my insurance rates were.

A WEEK AFTER Mary Ann Winkowski was born, her grandmother bathed her in red wine, not only to ward off the evil eye but to keep the devil away. It was an old Italian custom. Mary Ann's grandmother, Maria, was from the old country, a place where a targeted glance could ruin a person in many different ways and precautions needed to be taken. Evil spirits and curses weren't just the stuff of old wives' tales, but things to be taken seriously. Baptism would protect the baby more securely from the ravages of Old Scratch, but something had to be done in the interim between the birth and the blessing by the priest with holy water.

Maria had a gift. She saw things other people couldn't and could communicate with spirits of the deceased, mostly relatives or people she knew personally. Mary Ann's mother didn't disbelieve any of this, but she didn't have the ability her mother had, and as the baby grew to be a toddler, both were curious to see whether a special talent would manifest itself. The gift had been known to skip a generation.

The family didn't have to wait too long. When Mary Ann was two years old she saw and spoke to her first ghost. Her mother was in the hospital giving birth to her sister, and Mary Ann was staying with her grandmother. The young girl, who was verbally advanced for her age, began having a conversation with an invisible person standing in the corner. Maria questioned her about it, and the information Mary Ann relayed wasn't anything a two-year-old could possibly know. The gift had shown itself and, by the age of four, Mary Ann began visiting funeral homes on a regular basis to talk to the dead and help relatives deal with the loss of loved ones, and sometimes, not-so-loved ones.

I finished *When Ghosts Speak* a few days after Grace and Charlie came home from the hospital. I had expected to read the rantings of some over-the-top guru who went ghostbusting with a vacuum cleaner and a Ouija board, but it wasn't like that at all. Mary Ann, a married mother of two and a devoted Catholic who lived outside Cleveland, Ohio, sounded perfectly sane. More sane than I had felt in recent months. She had a no-nonsense approach to the supernatural and spoke in down-to-earth language about topics that could otherwise rocket into the stratosphere. Reading Mary Ann's book was like sitting at a kitchen table and eating cookies and drinking milk with your mom. Ghosts, or as she called them, earthbound spirits, were real. For her there was no question about that. She could see them the way she saw living people. Most of them were rather ordinary. Yes, they could move things or cause sounds to happen—sometimes they could cause temperatures to drop in a room—but they couldn't fly around or float through windows, couldn't predict the future or cast spells and most of the time they couldn't hurt you.

An earthbound spirit's personality was really determined by how the dead person had lived his life. If he was a kind person when he was alive, he was probably kind, albeit a bit disoriented, dead. If he was a jerk, well, most of the time dying didn't change that and you'd have a jerky ghost hanging around sometimes causing trouble. Most people who died went to the other side, wherever that was. The ones that stayed behind either had unfinished business with the living or were lost and needed someone to show them the way to what she called the white light (these were usually people who were terrible with directions in real life . . . kidding). Okay, the white light stuff sounded a little woo-woo to me, but God had been described as light for centuries, so why not? Maybe some souls just needed a little guidance to show them where they needed to go.

Maybe that's what was going on in our house. Maybe a ghost was like a fly.

Have you ever opened your car door and unwittingly let in a giant horsefly? You start up the ignition, pull out of your driveway, and soon thereafter you hear a buzzing and see something quickly fly in front of you and then disappear. It then circles and bumps into the driver's-side window and falls down, crawls on the door handle, and then flies again, this time wedging itself where the windshield meets the dashboard. It crawls around now, maybe moves a remnant of a child's thrown french fry, shakes up a bit of dust, and flies again. It can see the outside, but there is no way out. Then you open the window and the horsefly takes off and you never see it again.

Could it be that ghosts were like trapped flies and all they needed was someone to open a window for them?

I STILL HAD Mary Ann's phone number on a Post-it note in my wallet. I decided that I wanted to make the call after all, so one night I talked it over with Grace, who asked me why I wanted to do this. I asked if she had still been seeing shadows, and she admitted she had, but she believed that it was probably just a symptom from her pregnancy.

"And Eddie is still not wanting to go into his room?"

"He's anxious about the baby, that's all."

"And the toys?"

"We already went over this."

"What about the time we heard the glass break in the living room?"

"Well, I'll give you that one. I got nothing for that."

"See?"

I asked her what the big deal was, and it took her a moment before she said that her grandmother had told her never to fool around with this sort of thing. If there was something in the house and it wasn't bothering anyone, just leave it alone.

"But it's bothering me," I said. "And it's bothering Eddie."

"We don't know it's bothering Eddie. He's just a little boy and he doesn't want to be alone."

"But he won't even go in the room *with* us."

She said nothing. She was tired and, in retrospect, I probably shouldn't have approached her with this so soon after she had given birth, but I needed to do something and not just read books.

"I just want to do this."

"Doesn't it go against being Catholic if you make this call?"

She had me there.

In the famous Witch of Endor story in the first book of Samuel in the Old Testament, Saul, the first king of the Hebrews, is in a very precarious situation. He is about to have his ass handed to him by the Philistines. He prays to God and, getting no answer, decides to visit a medium and trick her into conjuring the prophet Samuel, who had recently died. It was against Jewish law to conjure the dead, and the penalty was stoning.

> When Saul saw the camp of the Philistines, he was dismayed and lost heart completely.
>
> He therefore consulted the LORD; but the LORD gave no answer, whether in dreams or by the Urim or through prophets.
>
> Then Saul said to his servants, "Find me a woman who is a medium, to whom I can go to seek counsel through her." His servants answered him, "There is a woman in Endor who is a medium."
>
> So he disguised himself, putting on other clothes, and set out with two companions. They came to the woman by night, and Saul said to her, "Tell my fortune through a ghost; conjure up for me the one I ask you to."
>
> But the woman answered him, "You are surely aware of what Saul has done, in driving the mediums and fortune-tellers out of the land. Why, then, are you laying snares for my life, to have me killed?"

But Saul swore to her by the LORD, "As the LORD lives, you shall incur no blame for this."

Then the woman asked him, "Whom do you want me to conjure up?" and he answered, "Samuel."

When the woman saw Samuel, she shrieked at the top of her voice and said to Saul, "Why have you deceived me? You are Saul!"

But the king said to her, "Have no fear. What do you see?" The woman answered Saul, "I see a preternatural being rising from the earth."

"What does he look like?" asked Saul. And she replied, "It is an old man who is rising, clothed in a mantle." Saul knew that it was Samuel, and so he bowed face to the ground in homage.

Samuel then said to Saul, "Why do you disturb me by conjuring me up?" Saul replied, "I am in great straits, for the Philistines are waging war against me and God has abandoned me. Since he no longer answers me through prophets or in dreams, I have called you to tell me what I should do."

To this Samuel said, "But why do you ask me, if the LORD has abandoned you and is with your neighbor?

The LORD has done to you what he foretold through me: he has torn the kingdom from your grasp and has given it to your neighbor David.

Because you disobeyed the LORD's directive and

would not carry out his fierce anger against Amalek, the LORD has done this to you today.

Moreover, the LORD will deliver Israel, and you as well, into the clutches of the Philistines. By tomorrow you and your sons will be with me, and the LORD will have delivered the army of Israel into the hands of the Philistines."

Immediately Saul fell full length on the ground, for he was badly shaken by Samuel's message (1 Samuel 28:5–20).

Things didn't turn out too well for Saul after that, and though stoning has gone out of fashion in most of the world, throughout Church history consulting a medium to invoke the dead was seen as a grievous sin.

Why is conjuring so bad? Well, for starters, if a person believes in God, then that person needs to put complete trust in God. Contacting a psychic to find out about the future means that you're anxious in some way about the future, which is a completely normal emotion. But ultimately God doesn't want you to worry about such things. God will provide, and your wanting to know what's going to happen tomorrow indicates doubt.

Second, it can be dangerous. As Pope Paul VI said, we know very little about the spirit world. It's not that the Church denies the existence of an invisible world, it just warns against getting involved in any of it for the simple reason there is no rule book. No one knows how an unseen world works. Nor do people have any idea of what they are getting themselves involved in, which is why it's a no-no to play with a Ouija board.

Imagine for a moment that you sign up for an online dating service. You log in and over the course of a few weeks you begin to meet some people. Most of them seem too strange or boring for you, but then one person really seems to stand out. That person is good-looking and funny and has a lot in common with you. When you chat online, you have a great time, and unlike some of the other weirdos you've talked to in the past, this person leaves you alone. Gives you space. He or she isn't a stalker and isn't constantly bombarding you with e-mails asking how you are or forwarding you chain letters. Soon, you begin to feel at ease and share some of your innermost thoughts. You begin to really open up to the person on the other side of cyberspace.

After a couple of months your friend suggests it's about time the two of you meet. You agree. You're excited to finally see this person face-to-face, this person to whom you're really attracted and who has, in a very short time, etched a place in your heart. So you agree to meet at a restaurant for dinner somewhere. The night finally arrives. You get all dressed up. You can't wait and all day you're buzzing around in anticipation. As you're getting out of the car you notice a frightening individual walking toward you. This person introduces him- or herself as your friend, even though he or she doesn't look anything like the person you've seen in pictures or in your imagination. This person then takes out a sledgehammer, smashes you in the head, drags your body into a car, drives away, and buries you in a basement somewhere in Canada.

Kind of like that.

Same applies for conjuring spirits. The truth is, you can never know for sure exactly who or what you are talking to. You may think the spirit that you encounter is kindhearted and benign, or even angelic, but you just never know.

I SAT THERE for a moment and rolled Grace's question around in my head: Doesn't it go against being Catholic if you make this call?

No, I reasoned. I wasn't conjuring a spirit. The ghost was already here and if anything, it was conjuring me in its weird little ghost world. I just wanted confirmation it was here. I wasn't going to etch a pentagram into the floor to call it forth and ask for its assistance in ruling the world. All I wanted to know is what *it* wanted and to get *it* the hell out of here.

"Don't worry about that," I said to her. "Plus, have you heard some of the language that has come out of my mouth in recent years? I think those things trump this."

"Good point," she said. She paused for a moment. Charlie, who had been sleeping in his crib in the dining room, began crying. "Fine," she said. "Go ahead."

The following day I called Mary Ann and left a message on her answering machine. I gave her my name, mentioned Peggy, and told her that I was the editor at QPB and that we were excited to be offering her book in paperback to members in the upcoming months. Then I asked her if she wouldn't mind calling me back because I thought I had a ghost in my house (I couldn't believe I said that to someone I didn't even know). I then hung up and waited for her to ring me back.

IN HIS BOOK *Everything You Ever Wanted to Know About Heaven but Never Dreamed of Asking!*, Peter Kreeft, a professor of philosophy at Boston College, well-respected theologian, and one of only a few people in recent years to talk about things that go bump in the night from a Catholic perspective, writes that there are three types of ghosts:

> First, the most familiar kind: the sad ones, the wispy ones. They seem to be working out some unfinished earthly business or suffering some purgatorial purification until released from their earthly business. . . .
>
> Second there are the malicious and deceptive spirits—and since they are deceptive, they hardly ever appear

malicious. These are probably the ones who respond to conjuring at séances. They probably come from Hell. . . .

Third, there are the bright, happy spirits of dead friends and family, especially spouses, who appear unbidden, at God's will, not ours, with messages of hope and love.

While I was sure Kreeft knew what he was talking about, wouldn't a spirit from hell not be a ghost at all, but a demon? At one time, ghosts would have been human, and a human couldn't become an angel because an angel was a totally different species. The way a cat could never become a dog, and a supermodel could never become an angel no matter what Victoria's Secret said. Were there really damned human souls, and could they wreak havoc in our material world?

Moreover, Kreeft left off his list the poltergeist, or noisy spirit, like the one Father Herbert Thurston wrote about in his book *Ghosts and Poltergeists*. He defined a poltergeist as a "racketing spirit, which in almost all cases remains invisible but which manifests its presence by throwing things about, knocking fire irons together and creating an uproar, in the course of which the human spectators are occasionally hit by flying objects, but as a rule suffer no serious injury."

And then there seemed to be ghosts that suffered some type of tragedy and didn't know they were dead, or didn't want to move on to the next stage of life after death.

As I waited for Mary Ann to call, I thought about which type of spirit might be in our house. Was it sad, angry, demonic, or some kind of poltergeist in training? I tried to put the idea out of my head and did so by praying the Rosary, asking God and the Blessed Mother for protection if it was necessary.

A couple of days had passed and we hadn't heard from Mary Ann. Peggy had said she had a waiting list, but in the last forty-eight hours I had started to get cold feet. There hadn't been much activity in the house since the baby came home. Maybe Grace had been right. If there was something here, it hadn't harmed us—certainly, it had been disturbing, at least to me, and possibly to Eddie too, but maybe it was because we just didn't understand what was going on. I began to feel sorry for it, without knowing what *it* was.

On the third night, the phone rang and an Ohio number showed up on caller ID. I grabbed the phone and a pen and paper to take notes and, without knowing why, ran upstairs to Eddie's room, which I hadn't entered during the past couple of weeks. I rested myself near my son's dresser and clicked the phone to talk.

"Is this Gary?"

"Yes."

"It's Mary Ann Winkowski, how are you?"

She had a wonderful, warm Midwestern accent and instantly, any sense of trepidation that I had felt over the last few days melted away. With just a few little words I felt like I had known this woman my entire life.

We talked for five minutes about her book and how much I liked it. She said she was so happy with the responses she had received from so many people. She had been nervous about how it would be received, but she had gotten dozens of letters telling her how much the book had helped, and was glad she had written it. She was so sweet and genuine and I could have talked with her for hours, but we eventually got down to business.

She explained to me that she had the ability to determine if there was a ghost in a house by either being there in person or by listening over the phone, but the call needed to be made from a landline. Cell phones didn't work for whatever reason. And since she was nearly five hundred miles away, she was going to give me a phone reading.

I told her I was ready. I had revealed almost nothing about myself. All she knew was my name, where I worked, and my phone number (which was unlisted and my address wasn't available on the Internet or in the white pages). There was silence on the phone for a few seconds, and then she started asking me questions.

"Is there a yellow room in your house?"

"Yes."

"And that room has no closets, correct?"

"Right."

"And does a child live in that room?"

"Yes."

"And it's your son, right?"

"Right."

She paused for a minute. I was impressed, especially about nailing the color of the room and the fact that it didn't have a closet.

"Okay, now, who's Maryanne?"

"Well, that's you."

"No, there's another Maryanne."

"Oh," I said, "that's my sister."

"Did she get hurt in that room?"

"Oh my God, she did. She accidently fell and cut her wrist on something sharp when she was a kid. I was a Boy Scout at the time and I butterflied the wound. To this day, she says I saved her life."

"Who's Merrick?"*

I paused for a minute and thought. I didn't know any Merrick at all. "I don't know," I said. "You mean a person? A person named Merrick?"

"I think so," she said. "That's not coming through clearly, but I'm really getting Merrick."

"Are you sure it's a person?" I asked. "There's a town named Merrick about six miles from my house."

---

*For purposes of privacy, I have changed this name.

"I don't know," Mary Ann said. "I'm just picking up Merrick. I feel like it's a name, but I could be wrong."

She paused again and then asked, "Your house is over a hundred years old, right?"

"Yes."

"And is there a glass box in the downstairs near a big picture window in the front of your house?"

"Well, as a matter of fact there is a glass box by the window," I said. "Wow, you're good."

"I know," she laughed before continuing. "It's a tall box, with glass on three sides, right?

"Well, yes it is. You have access to some military satellite or something? My wife keeps these special plates in the box. She loves those plates."

There was silence over the phone and Mary Ann was murmuring softly to herself.

"So, what do you think?" I finally asked.

"Well," she said in a long way, resting on the double *l* at the end of the word. "You have a couple of things going on in your house," Mary Ann had replied.

"A couple?"

"Yes, you have a woman, an older woman. She's short, with short hair. She stays downstairs for the most part. She's been in your house a long time. A very long time. She was dead when your house was built. You've lived in the house a long time, haven't you?"

"Yes," I said.

"Since you were a child, right?"

"Yes."

"She was around when you were young. She likes to stay in the front room of your house by the picture window. She walks back and forth from the room to the front door, which is right next to the room. It's as if she's waiting for someone. She's standing next to the glass box right now."

The hairs on the back of my neck started to stand up on end.

"Oh my God, are you serious?" I said. A time machine in my head raced back to the night in the kitchen when I was seven years old and my mom told me of the ghost woman looking out the window waiting for someone to return.

"My mom said there was a ghost in our house growing up and she described her the same way," I said. "Mary Ann, *she described her the very same way.* I never really believed her."

She had given a short laugh and said, "You should have listened to your mother." Then her voice changed slightly and there was a seriousness in her tone that hadn't been there before.

"Yes. She's very low energy. I'm not concerned about her."

"What?"

"I'm not concerned about her."

"What? Wait, you said there were two ghosts in the

house? And if you just said that you're not worried about the woman . . ." I didn't finish my sentence.

"Well, you have another ghost, a man. He's younger than the woman and he's been in your house only about a year. Him, I don't like. I don't like him at all. He's a bit of a troublemaker."

"He's *what*?"

"And Gary?"

"Yes?" And just as I answered her, I felt that electric surge run up and down my body.

"He's standing right on top of you now."

Chapter 9

People from all walks of life have encountered ghosts: from common people whose names are lost to history, to Saint Augustine, who writes about a haunted house in the miracles section of the twenty-second book of *The City of God*; from Abraham Lincoln to Sir Arthur Conan Doyle, the creator of Sherlock Holmes, to Joan Rivers. Dee Snider, from the rock group Twisted Sister, was visited by the ghost of his deceased brother-in-law. (Dee grew up in Baldwin, the next town over.) Even Jesus was visited by a ghost.

I'm not kidding.

In Luke 9:28–36 there is the story of Jesus and his unique camping trip on a mountain.

About eight days after he said this, he took Peter, John, and James and went up the mountain to pray.

While he was praying his face changed in appearance and his clothing became dazzling white.

And behold, two men were conversing with him, Moses and Elijah, who appeared in glory and spoke of his exodus that he was going to accomplish in Jerusalem.

Peter and his companions had been overcome by sleep, but becoming fully awake, they saw his glory and the two men standing with him.

As they were about to part from him, Peter said to Jesus, "Master, it is good that we are here; let us make three tents, one for you, one for Moses, and one for Elijah." But he did not know what he was saying.

While he was still speaking, a cloud came and cast a shadow over them, and they became frightened when they entered the cloud.

Then from the cloud came a voice that said, "This is my chosen Son; listen to him."

After the voice had spoken, Jesus was found alone. They fell silent and did not at that time tell anyone what they had seen.

Did you see the ghost? It's Moses. He had been dead for a long time (Elijah is a bit of a freak and doesn't count as a ghost—he supposedly never died but rode off to the great beyond in a chariot of fire). And why didn't Jesus' friends say anything to anyone? Because no one would believe them, that's why. Even then, people were suspicious of ghosts.

Now, no matter what you feel about Jesus, whether you like him, don't like him, are totally ambivalent, think he looks good as a plastic statue on the dashboard of your car, you have to hand it to him—he was an amazing storyteller. His parables, which were atomically powered short stories that he told to get people to think, are not only etched in the collective psyche of Catholics around the world, but are ingrained in Western culture as well. Stories like the parables of the Good Samaritan and the Prodigal Son cross all faiths and creeds.

But did you know that Jesus liked a good ghost story, too? Maybe that encounter with the ghost of Moses had some effect on his storytelling. Who knows? But the tale isn't found in any of the gnostic gospels or one of those suddenly uncovered scrolls *National Geographic* keeps in a metal desk in a warehouse somewhere in order to make a documentary for sweeps week. It's found, again, in the Bible.

Later on in the Gospel of Luke 16:19–31, Jesus gathers his followers around and tells them the story of Lazarus and the Rich Man.

There was a rich man who dressed in purple garments and fine linen and dined sumptuously each day.

And lying at his door was a poor man named Lazarus, covered with sores, who would gladly have eaten his fill of the scraps that fell from the rich man's table. Dogs even used to come and lick his sores.

When the poor man died, he was carried away by angels to the bosom of Abraham. The rich man also died and was buried, and from the netherworld, where he was in torment, he raised his eyes and saw Abraham far off and Lazarus at his side.

And he cried out, "Father Abraham, have pity on me. Send Lazarus to dip the tip of his finger in water and cool my tongue, for I am suffering torment in these flames."

Abraham replied, "My child, remember that you received what was good during your lifetime while Lazarus likewise received what was bad; but now he is comforted here, whereas you are tormented.

Moreover, between us and you a great chasm is established to prevent anyone from crossing who might wish to go from our side to yours or from your side to ours."

He said, "Then I beg you, father, send him to my father's house, for I have five brothers, so that he may warn them, lest they too come to this place of torment."

But Abraham replied, "They have Moses and the prophets. Let them listen to them."

He said, "Oh no, father Abraham, but if someone from the dead goes to them, they will repent."

Then Abraham said, "If they will not listen to Moses and the prophets, neither will they be persuaded if someone should rise from the dead."

Did you catch it? The poor rich man who blew his chance in life asked Abraham to help him out and send Lazarus, a good spirit, a ghost if you will, to the living, to impart a message to his brothers, to shake them up and force them to change the path they were on (sounds a lot like the exchange between Jacob Marley and Ebenezer Scrooge in Charles Dickens's *A Christmas Carol*). Abraham, because he's kind of badass, refuses. He doesn't think it would do them any good. He didn't say it couldn't be done, just that it wasn't going to happen now. Makes you wonder if the great patriarch would have agreed to a haunting if the rich man's brothers had felt something like a lightning bolt coursing through their spines.

"OH MY GOD," I cried out. I could feel the surge of electricity running throughout my body. "Mary Ann, I can feel it. It's like he's all over me."

"Yeah, he's not all that happy with you."

"With me? *What did I do?*"

"Yep, not too happy." And then she had added, "Oh,

he's been frightening your son. Your son doesn't want to sleep in his room anymore, does he?"

"No!" I blurted out. "What is it? Is it the devil?"

"Oh, no, it's not the devil, honey. It's not a demon. I can't see those types of spirits. I can only see the spirits of people who were once alive. And this one was definitely alive. He's twenty years old.* He's only been dead about a year and has been in your house for about the same amount of time."

"So, wait, is the woman ghost evil, too?"

"No, she's not evil. She's not bad at all. And the man isn't evil, either. He's not a bad guy, he's just mischievous. He knows he shouldn't be doing what he's doing, but he does it anyway."

"What am I supposed to do?"

"Well, whatever you do, *don't talk to them*."

"Don't talk to them? I have ghosts in my house and I can't talk to them?"

"Honey, didn't you read my book? If you talk to them, you give them power, so don't acknowledge them. Ignore them as much as possible."

"That's it? How do I get rid of them?"

"How far are you from Cleveland?"

"I don't know, like ten hours by car, maybe."

---

*For purposes of privacy, I have changed the man's age.

"Are you near Baltimore?

"No, that's about four hours away."

"Oh, that's too far. I'm going to be in Baltimore next week at the Edgar Allan Poe house to see what's hanging around there and thought if you were near there I could stop by."

"So what do I do?"

"Give me your address and I'm going to send you something in the mail. It's a smudge stick. All it is is sage and sweetgrass. It's a Native American thing. What you're going to do is take the stick, light it on fire, but do so in a pan or on a plate. I don't want you burning your house down. Then you put the flame out and what's going to happen is that the stick is going to smoke. Wait, do you have allergies?"

"No."

"Good. But you have small children, right? You better have them and your wife stay at someone's house for the night while you do it. The smell can be really powerful."

I told her I would do that.

"So once you have a nice bit of smoke coming out of the stick, I want you to start at the top of the house. You have an attic, right?"

"Yes."

"Start in the attic and I want you to say the Lord's Prayer and outline all the windows and doors in your house. Every one of them. Your closets, the doors to any rooms, the doors that lead in and out of your house. You have three doors that lead into your house, don't you?"

"No, two."

"Are you sure? I'm getting three."

I thought for a moment. "Oh, you're right. I think there's a doorway behind one of the walls that was covered over with drywall back when the washroom was added to the house. I saw it when I gutted the room after Grace and I moved in here a few years ago."

"That might be it, but I'm getting something else. Do you have an old mirror in the house? One that wasn't originally yours?"

She was right again. There was a creepy old vanity mirror in the downstairs bathroom that my father had fished out of the garbage years ago and brought home one day. My mom hated it, but my dad had installed it in the bathroom anyway. I had never gotten around to changing it after Grace and I moved in.

"Yes," I answered. "How do you do this?"

She just laughed. "It's what I do, honey."

"What about the mirror?"

"Well, you never know what the original owner might have done with that mirror or what kind of person it was who looked into it every day. Everything has energy and leaves behind traces of energy and that can build up in a mirror. Not only that, sometimes people use them in ceremonies to play with things they shouldn't play with. But don't worry about it."

"*What do you mean, don't worry about it?* How can I not worry about it? Just telling me not to worry is going to make me worry."

"It's going to be okay, honey. Don't worry. Now, do you have a lot of antiques in the house?"

"No."

"Stuff from garage sales?"

"No. Wait. Yes. Actually, we do. My mom still goes to garage sales and every time we visit she gives us things she's picked up. Usually religious things."

"Oh, that's not good. People just don't know what they are bringing into their houses when they do these things. I'm not saying you shouldn't have anything secondhand, but when we bring in other people's belongings, we sometimes bring in pieces of them, too. You never know what is attached to an object like a ring or a picture or a statue. You just don't know."

"It's kind of like a relic, just the opposite, right?"

"Exactly. The same principle. A relic is imbued with the holiness of the person who had carried it with them. Not everyone is as holy as the saints." She paused and then said, "This is what I want you to do. I want you to get a spray bottle, fill it with water and a tablespoon of sea salt, and then I want you to spray the corners of your house and these objects that have come into your house. Don't worry, by the time we're done, your house will be fine."

"And what does the smoke do again?"

"It's called smudging, and for whatever reason the smoke calms spirits down, basically drains them of their energy. It's going to help them cross over. We need to calm them down so they can go into the light."

"Kind of like when a priest burns incense at a funeral. He's helping the spirit rise to heaven, toward God's light."

She laughed. "Oh, you're good, honey. That's just right." Then she asked, "Have you had your house blessed?"

"Yes, a couple years ago. But wait, why wouldn't that have gotten rid of the woman spirit downstairs?"

"A priest needs to know what he's blessing. When he just gives a general blessing, he's basically just blessing the spirit, too."

"Can I ask you one more question?"

"Sure you can."

"Why are the ghosts here?"

"Oh, honey, I don't know. They're not talking to me now. It's not that they won't at some later time, but they're not saying anything right now. Sometimes ghosts just go where there is a lot of energy. Sometimes people invite them in like bringing an object into a house that has one attached to it. It's hard to say. Sometimes there's a reason and sometimes there isn't."

I realized that as we were talking the electric sensation had gone away and I hadn't even noticed it.

I gave Mary Ann my address, thanked her, and we agreed to talk again after I had smudged the house so she could give me the next steps for clearing the ghosts out. I hung up the phone and replayed our conversation in my head, filling out the notes I had taken while we were talking.

I was overwhelmed. I believed her and while it may sound naïve that I gave myself over to what she was saying so easily, I felt a certain peace move through me that I hadn't felt in a year.

I went downstairs and told Grace that I had a great conversation with Mary Ann, that she was warm and pleasant and funny, and I felt like she was my second mom. Grace asked me what she had said, and I told her I would tell her after the kids went to sleep.

"YOU MEAN TO TELL ME there are two ghosts in the house?"

"That's what she said." I had told her everything Mary Ann relayed to me, and she sat patiently and listened.

"And you believe her?"

"I do."

"So what are we supposed to do?"

I told her about the plan to clean the house by smudging it.

"I don't like that."

"What's the big deal? Priests do it at funerals. What do you think they're doing when they shake the smoke from an incense burner around a casket?"

"But you're not a priest. What are you going to do, start blessing Ritz crackers and giving Communion, too?"

Ouch. She got me on that one.

"Everything will be okay. I promise."

She looked at me and I realized she wasn't angry. She was frightened.

"Look, I'm not saying you shouldn't believe her. Maybe she's right. I just don't like these sorts of things."

I nodded my head, but at this point I was convinced and ready to do whatever Mary Ann said. I looked at Grace, and, invoking Indiana Jones, said, "Trust me."

That night I thought about my mom and her stories of angels, and the ghost that lived in our house. She was never the same after the murder of Christopher Gruhn—it was like the devil had stolen a part of her soul. For fifty days the police searched for his killer and during that time my mother wept and hardly spoke a word to us. I knew inside she somehow blamed herself. She had a vision like she had had on many different occasions and had seen something in her head, something terrible, and didn't know how to interpret it or what to do. In the weeks that followed, she reached out to some of the priests and nuns in our community to talk about what had happened and about the visions she had seen. But they didn't understand what she was talking about or know how to even deal with her. Some of them were sympathetic and listened patiently. Others thought she needed a psychiatrist. Still others told her that visions weren't real. I wanted to help her, but I didn't know what to do, either. I tried to pay attention to her during the times she came out of her shell, but I wasn't any help to her. I could tell she needed an answer, but there were no answers to be found, at least not from any of us. Eventually, my mom stopped talking about everything and retreated into herself. I know she felt abandoned by God, left alone by the one person she loved more than anything in this world. And though she never told me this, I'm sure she felt abandoned by me as well.

In the days after the murder, Rockville Centre was a veritable ghost town at night. Children stayed home with their parents, curtains and blinds were drawn. The people in grocery stores seemed to move about quickly and didn't make eye contact with each other. Cop cars roamed the streets in the evenings in a way they never had before. No one knew who could have done such a thing or if that person was going to strike again. People talked about how this sort of thing never happened in Rockville Centre. But they were wrong.

On May 10, 1983, seventeen-year-old Robert W. Golliver was arrested and a year later convicted of murder. He had lived two doors away from Christopher Gruhn.

THE DAY AFTER I SPOKE to Mary Ann on the phone, I called Peggy to tell her everything that had happened and, though she was excited to hear the story, she couldn't speak long on the phone. I then called a friend of mine at another publish-. ing house who I knew loved this sort of thing and related to her the events of the previous night. She was a firm believer in the paranormal, and while we were on the phone she did a quick Google search for any links that might bring together some of this information Mary Ann had relayed to me. After a few minutes she said, "I found your ghost. Well, at least one of them. Here, I'm going to send it to you."

I waited a moment, watched her e-mail appear on my computer screen, clicked it open, and read the story of a twenty-year-old man named Peter Smith who was involved in a car accident on March 7, 2007. He had lost control of his car and plowed into another vehicle, injuring the driver. Later that night, he was pronounced dead at a local hospital, not too far away from where I lived. I read the article again quickly and that's when I noticed something that sent chills up my spine. The man was from Merrick.*

My mouth dropped open. I didn't know what to think. It was uncanny. This seemed to fit what Mary Ann had told me on the phone. And it fit the timeframe. I had started experiencing the strange sensation in Eddie's room in early March of that year and though Merrick wasn't the guy's name, it had been the place he had lived. Was I just grabbing at straws or could this man's spirit actually be in my house? I didn't know Peter Smith and was positive I had never met him, but something seemed strangely familiar about it all—I just didn't know what.

"It's eerie," my friend said. "It fits everything."

"Yeah, I started feeling things in the house in March . . ." A wave of panic rushed over me.

"My God," I said. "This does say March 7, right?"

"Yeah, why? What's March 7?"

"I don't know. I'll call you back."

I hung up the phone and quickly dialed Grace. She picked up after the first ring. I didn't know how to say this, so I just started.

"Grace, I'm sorry, but I have to ask you something."

---

*This incident really happened. I have changed the name of the victim and his age and substituted a different nearby town to protect the family's privacy. But it is important to note that this substitution is consistent with the changes made on pages 142 and 152. The actual age and the word Mary Ann Winkowski used during our initial phone conversation were the same age and word in the article I read that day in my office.

"What?" she said.

"When did you miscarry?"

"Last year. Why?"

"No, I know last year, but when last year?"

"In March. What's this all about?"

"March what?"

"Hold on. I still have the paperwork."

She put the phone down and I waited, rereading the article that was on my computer. Why did all of this sound so familiar and why was I mildly freaking out right now?

"Okay, I have it here."

"What does it say?"

"March 7, 2007."

"And when was Charlie supposed to be born? What was his due date?"

"March 7, 2008." She had paused. "I never realized they were the same date. That's weird."

I stared at the article on the screen and closed my eyes and said, "It's going to get even weirder."

PART III

Dearly Departed

Remember, O Lord, the God of Spirits and of all Flesh, those whom
we have remembered and those whom we have not remembered.
—Liturgy of Saint James

Chapter 10

The transmigration of souls is an idea shared by many cultures and religions around the world. Otherwise known as reincarnation, it is a belief that when the spirit separates from the body at the time of death, it roams around for a while and eventually makes its way back to Earth in the form of a baby. The belief in karma—or the balance sheet of good versus bad deeds that determines what happens to you after you die—and in *samsara*, or the wheel of rebirth, is prevalent in Hinduism and Buddhism, though versions exist in other religions as well.

In Vedic traditions, the ever-spinning wheel contains six states of incarnation: gods; elemental forces like wind and fire; humans; animals; the frightening pretas, or "hungry ghosts," purgatorial creatures bound by their unfulfilled desires to roam the world until something breaks the cycle; and citizens of hell, which unlike Christianity's version, is a temporal place, kind of a harsher purgatory. Though the idea isn't found in major sects of Judaism today, *gilgul* is the mystical Hebrew term used in kabbalah that means transmigration of one soul to another body. Even early gnostic Christians believed in the concept, citing the passage in the gospel of Matthew where Jesus referred to John the Baptist as being the new Elijah (though mentioning a belief in reincarnation today is enough to get your ass kicked to the curb at your local church).

I never really thought much about reincarnation. As a Catholic, I believed that everyone who ever lived was a brand-new creation, right off the lot without any used parts. But what did happen to a soul once it separated from its body? Did it travel some spiritual superhighway greater than the speed of light to get to its next destination? If a lot of people died on the same day, was there traffic like on the Long Island Expressway on a Friday afternoon? Could souls cross paths, swap stories, and visit one another's relatives, just to check in and look in on them?

All these questions and ideas swirled around in my head as I waited over the next few days for Mary Ann's package to arrive. I would wake every morning and pray the Rosary and ask the Blessed Mother to help me understand all of this. If Peter Smith's ghost was in our house, was it just a coincidence that he had died on the same day that Grace miscarried? And was it just a coincidence that Charlie was supposed to be born on the same day a year later? I thought of Pope John Paul II, who had said that there was no such thing as a coincidence. If there wasn't, then what was going on? All of this was unsettling to Grace and brought back bad memories of the past year. She didn't know what to believe and, to be honest, I didn't, either.

The house had been quiet for the last few days. Eddie still stayed away from his bedroom, but there had been no strange sounds or noises, no minor electrical disturbances, no stray shadows. Everything seemed peaceful in a way that it hadn't in some time. Granted, the four of us were all sleeping in the same bedroom and Charlie was waking us up in the middle of night three or four times, but that was normal.

The box arrived the following week and inside it were two six-inch-long bushels of sage and sweetgrass tied together with string. Upon seeing all this, Grace started shaking her head at me. "Do you really want to do this? You're going to set yourself on fire," she said.

I was nervous and perplexed and wanted to get it over and done with, but I have to admit I was curious about what was going to happen. Would there be any change to the house? Would I actually see a spirit materialize? Would I get slimed like Bill Murray in *Ghostbusters*? I wanted to find out, and I wanted to find out fast.

I assured her everything would be fine, but she wasn't convinced.

"So what are you going to be doing? Performing an exorcism or something?"

"I don't know. I never thought of it like that. Mary Ann said it would help them cross over, but I guess it's like an exorcism. I mean Mary Ann said they weren't evil, so maybe it's not an exorcism. I just don't know."

"I know you want to become a deacon someday, but you don't know what you're doing. Don't you think you should have a priest do this?"

I was insulted. Maybe she was right. Maybe I was playing with something I shouldn't have been playing with, but I didn't care. Hubris welled up inside me. We had had a priest in our house some years back, and if his blessing hadn't gotten rid of an old woman ghost, who was to say that it would do any good now? I stared at her in a moment of defiance before I said, "I'm going to do it myself."

INCENSE, according to theologian John Hardon, is an "aromatic gum or resin in the form of powder or grains that give off a fragrant smoke when they are burned. When blessed it is a symbolic sacramental. Its burning signifies zeal or fervor; its fragrance, virtue; its rising smoke, human prayers ascending to God."

While what I was lighting near the stove wasn't incense, it sure had a powerful smell and I imagined the ghosts sniffing it and busting out bongs, relaxing on some spectral futon, thanking me for the "good smokes" with a mellow "Groovy, man."

Grace and the boys were staying at her mother's and I started having second thoughts as the flame began to overtake the stick. I was alone and I had told Grace I was going to do this myself, but that had been only a half-truth. I was frightened and had no idea what I was getting myself in to. I couldn't admit that to Grace, but I didn't want to do this alone. I had called a few people earlier in the day to see if they would stay with me while I smoked my house. That was when I realized I had no friends. People either didn't call me back or, if they did, they would say something like, "Hey man, I would love to help you, but my wife doesn't want me bringing anything home with me, so I have to pass."

Cowards.

I put the smudge stick out by tapping it against an aluminum saucepan, and the smoke billowed out of it. I left it by the stove and wandered around the house aimlessly for a little while. Nervous habit. I felt like my grandmother's old dog, Puppy (that was his name), a one-eyed, broken-tailed pooch with a rocking case of halitosis who would walk around in circles when he was anxious (and occasionally hit his head on the blind side). But it wasn't just me. The house had a stifling heaviness about it, and that made me feel tense and uneasy, like I was being watched.

After a few minutes I went into the kitchen and grabbed the saucepan, the smudge stick, a box of matches, and my rosary, which I hung around my neck, and made the climb to the second floor. I heard every creak on every step and remembered my father telling me, when I was a boy, how old houses were as flatulent as old men. Well, this house had some gas and as I climbed higher I thought I saw a shadow move across the hallway toward the bathroom, but I quickly wrote it off as just my imagination (though I really wasn't sure that was the cause). I felt spooked and began reciting the Lord's Prayer in my head, but really, what was I worried about? I trusted Mary Ann. She told me the spirits weren't evil and I believed her. I had nothing to be afraid of, right?

I stood at the top of the stairs and everything seemed magnified—the light from the bathroom, the shadows in the corners, the sound of my clothes as I shifted my weight from one foot to the other. I stood for a moment trying to listen and heard nothing. I turned the handle and pulled the attic door open, a long witch-like screech coming from the hinge. I shook my head. "Nice," I thought. Then I wondered if I should go downstairs to get a can of WD-40. (I get easily distracted.) I walked up the stairs and, once at the top, struck a match and lit the stick.

I could feel my heart beating in my ears, and my shoulders were tall and tense. I held my breath for a moment and then, seeing and hearing and feeling nothing, I relaxed and exhaled. With a steady stream of smoke smoldering from the stick, I turned to the window that overlooked the north side of the house and looking out could see the arthritic-looking trees along Hillside Avenue naked and gray against a cold blue sky. I raised the stick and began outlining a box around the window, intoning, "Our Father, who art in heaven, hallowed be thy name," the sweet-smelling smoke rising around the window and up toward the ceiling.

I thought I heard something behind me and, turning, I looked to my left and to my right, half expecting to see something, a shadow, a person, a demon, a Smurf, anything. There were just boxes of clothes and old books in cases. I began walking slowly across the length of the attic and about halfway to the other side the smoke, which only moments before had been powerful and strong, went out. I thought it had just burned out, so I lit it again and could sense a shift in the room, a subtle chill. I walked to the window, looked out at the cathedral, changed the prayer to the Hail Mary, and outlined the window with smoke.

I walked back across the attic, descended the stairs, and began smudging each corner of every room and the windows and doorways as well. I was expecting Eddie's room to be a place of activity, but it was quiet. The wild sensation I had felt for so many months was nonexistent. I moved to the back room and did the same, praying and outlining doorways and windows. I did the master bedroom and all along the hallway as I made my way to the bathroom.

Just as I was about to cross through the doorway, the smudge stick went out again and I felt that sensation of cold electricity wash all over me. This time, it didn't just run up my back, it seemed to surround every part of me. I tried shaking it off as a wet dog would rain. The feeling was so intense and, ignoring what Mary Ann told me about talking to ghosts, I yelled out, "Get the hell off me!" Outside I heard a dog barking and I was sure it was just a coincidence, but the sound scared me even more than what was going on now. Trying to ignore everything around me, I smudged the windows, the door, and the mirror and then made my way downstairs.

I smoked the first floor of the house and went down to the basement. When I was done, I took the saucepan and what was left of the smudge stick and left it outside in the backyard. It had started to drizzle and I stood outside breathing in the rain and the fresh air. I smelled like a New Age barbecue, and as the rain started to pick up I went inside and walked around the house. Everything seemed quiet. I kept thinking about the incident in the bathroom and how intense the electric feeling had been. I was tired, so I lay down on the couch and fell asleep.

I wasn't asleep long, but when I woke up I remembered why the story of Peter Smith seemed so familiar.

JOHN HARDON ON CURSES:

A curse is to call down evil on someone or something.

In the Bible a curse is often a prayer of imprecation. Israelites knew that they could not constrain the Almighty but only move him by prayer. Unlike the magical incantations of their neighbors, the ancient Jews believed that Yahweh could remove a curse by his blessing, preserve the pious person from an undeserved curse, change the blessing of an unworthy priest into a curse, and turn aside a curse from a humble person because of meekness. In general, the intended evil of a curse takes effect only when the just God wills it.

I'm not sure I called evil down on someone, but I may have come close. Two days after Grace's miscarriage, I had come across a story about a man named Peter Smith from Merrick who two nights before had died when he lost control of his car. I had assumed from the report that he was speeding. Grace's miscarriage was in the forefront of my mind and as I read the story I grew more and more angry at the man for having been so reckless. Not only did he kill himself, but he could have killed another driver. I thought about the waste of life—and the lost life of the child Grace and I would never know—and I thought about the man's parents and the pain they must have been suffering knowing their son was dead. Had the man been married? Did he have a kid? I had no idea, but I remembered exclaiming out loud, "You idiot. What the hell were you thinking?" My words, flippant and stupid, were charged with vehemence.

Had Peter Smith's spirit heard what I said about him? Do thoughts and words travel in different ways in a ghost world? Or do words and thoughts have a power that we don't fully realize today? The ancients believed in the power of words to destroy and control, which is why in Judaism you are never allowed to say the name of God. Words have power. Thoughts have power. Maybe the idea of the *malocchio*, the evil eye, wasn't just a piece of superstition but was something real and true and destructive. Maybe every negative thought was like a spiritual attack aimed at another individual. Had my anger toward a total stranger somehow trapped this man in-between this world and the next? Was that why Mary Ann said he was unhappy with me? Was that why he had been haunting me? Even if everything Mary Ann had said was a good guess, there is no way she could have known I had done this. No one had heard me. I had been alone when I said it. Or had I? Had this man's spirit been standing right next to me? Had he come to escort the soul of Grace's unborn baby to another place? Had he come to comfort her? To comfort me? And had I turned on him with my lack of compassion? Or was he here for a totally different reason, one I hadn't even thought of?

Emotion welled up inside me. Not because I was frightened, but because I was so very sorry. That night I prayed for forgiveness, not to God, but to Peter Smith.

Chapter 11

The next morning I awoke, got dressed, and went off to get Grace and the boys. Even though they had only been gone half a day, I had missed them and wrapped my arms around Eddie for a long time and held Charlie next to me until it was time to leave his grandmother's.

When we arrived home, the house was quiet. It still smelled like sage and sweetgrass. Grace liked it. Eddie almost threw up, but after a few minutes he adjusted to it. Later that afternoon while the boys were taking a nap, I told Grace about everything that happened the day before.

"So you brought this stuff into our house?"

"I don't know. Maybe. It's not my fault."

"Yes, it is."

"Okay, you're right, but how was I supposed to know words have such power?"

"You work with books all the time, dingdong. You should know the power of words. Sticks and stones may break your bones, but words will send you to hell."

"Good point."

"So if we really do have ghosts in the house, does that mean they watch us all the time?"

"I don't know. I guess so."

"So that means they watch us in the bathroom."

"I guess so."

"Oh, that's gross." She was disgusted. "Could you just do whatever you have to do and get them out of here, please?"

"I'm working on it."

MARY ANN HAD TOLD ME to wait a couple of days after the smudging to give her a call. I did just that. Eddie was playing downstairs and Grace was cooking in the kitchen, so I went upstairs to the back room of the house that we use as a small reading room (though no one ever reads in it). I dialed her number and after a few rings she picked up. I said hello, asked how she was, and she talked to me about Baltimore and Edgar Allan Poe for a few minutes. Then she asked me how I did. I recounted the events of the day before, of how I began in the attic and worked my way down to the basement. She listened and asked if I had done all the windows and doors and all the corners and said all my prayers and I told her yes. I also told her how the smudge stick had gone out on two occasions.

"Oh, you hit them!" she exclaimed.

"Hit them?"

"Oh, you must have walked right up on them. The stick usually extinguishes when you find out where they are hiding. Didn't you read my book?"

"Yes, of course." But I didn't remember that part.

"At the end of the book I talked about the smudging and what might happen if you run into an earthbound spirit. I think maybe you ran into the man's spirit because he's not there right now."

"You mean he left the house? For good?"

"Well, I don't know. I don't think so. I'm just not picking up on him now. You know they come and they go sometimes. We just want to make sure that when they go, they really go, if you know what I mean." Mary Ann then asked me, "Are you upstairs on the second floor in the back of the house?"

"Yes," I said. How the heck did she know that?

"Oh, that's a strange room."

"Huh?"

"It has four doorways, doesn't it?"

"How could you possibly know that? Yes, it has four

doors. One for the closet, one for the back stairs that lead to the kitchen, one to the hallway, and one into my son Eddie's room."

"Oh, it's a gift, honey," she laughed. "And you're sitting on a couch, right?"

"Yes."

"Oh, interesting," she said, her voice trailing long at the end of the word.

"Okay, you scare me, Mary Ann, when you talk like that."

"I'm sorry, honey. It's just that man is back and the woman is around, too, and they are standing in the doorway that leads to your son's room."

"What?"

"Yep, they're standing right there."

"Why?"

"Well, they're a bit weak from the smudging. You know they don't like that sort of thing."

"So what, what do they want?"

"I don't know, they are just standing there."

"I know you said not to talk to them, but can I talk to them?"

"Well, you can if you want to."

"You'll interpret?"

"I'll try, honey."

"So what do I do, do I ask questions and then you'll be able to hear them?"

"If they answer, I will. The man is a still a bit upset with you but not as much as he was when you first called. The woman isn't upset at all. She just looks tired."

"So, wait, Mary Ann, I think I know his name."

"He says it's Peter."

I was flabbergasted. I told Mary Ann how my friend did a Google search and had found someone fitting the description of the guy. Merrick wasn't his name, it was the town he was from.

I felt the wave of electricity flow through me again, and Mary Ann replied, "He just left."

"Is he okay?"

"He's upset. I think he's getting ready to cross over. The lady kind of likes you, though. She's been around you for a very long time."

"Well, what's her name?"

"She's not saying. Wait, you said you were sitting on a couch, right?"

"Yes."

"There should be a box next to your couch. A cardboard box. What's in it?"

"Seriously, how do you do that, Mary Ann? I have one of those Staples storage boxes on the side of the couch."

"She's playing charades. She's having fun with you."

"Well, it's nice to know she likes to play games."

"Hmmmm, she keeps pointing to the box. What's inside the box?"

"Nothing. It's empty."

"Are you sure?"

I picked it up and turned it over. "Yep, nothing in it. Not even dust. Did I tell you what a clean house my wife keeps?"

"I'm sure she does." I could hear Mary Ann thinking. Slowly and softly, she repeated "box" over and over again. "Box, box, box. Wait! Her name is Box."

"Her name is Box? Like jack-in-the-box, Box?"

"Yes, Box."

"Are you sure?"

"Yes. She's nodding. It's Box!"

"I've never heard anyone with the name Box before. Is it her first name or her last name?"

"Last name."

"What's her first name?"

"She's smiling. She's enjoying this."

"Can she just tell me?"

"Nope. She wants you to find out."

"And how am I supposed to do that?"

"Keep playing, I guess. Oh, she's pointing to your couch now."

"So her name is Couch Box? She sounds like one of those hippies who used to live in this house. I thought you said she died around the turn of the century."

"No, her name isn't Couch. Wait, she wants you to guess a color. That's why she's pointing to the couch."

"Blue."

"Nope, that's not it."

"Yes, it is. It's a blue couch."

"She wants you to name another color."

"Another one? Really? I don't know, green?"

"Yes! Green. That's it. She's saying Green is it."

"So her name is Green Box?"

"No, no, no. Green is something else. Green is the place she's buried. She wants you to know where she's buried. It's someplace green."

"A cemetery."

"No. I mean, yes, a cemetery but one that has 'green' in its name."

"I don't know," I said. I tried to think. I was pretty familiar with most cemeteries on Long Island and Queens. My mom was the daughter of a grave digger, after all, and her idea of a good time was taking us to visit cemeteries on weekends. Sometimes we'd picnic there, but mostly, it was just afternoons spent wandering around the grounds looking for the spookiest tombstone we could find.

"Greenlawn?" I asked.

"No, that's not it?"

"Pinelawn? Pine is green."

"No, it's not Pinelawn."

"Wait, is she even buried around here?"

"She's saying yes. She's saying she didn't live around

here. She lived some towns away from you, but she's buried not far from your house."

"I don't know, Mary Ann. I'm pretty sure there aren't any cemeteries around here with 'green' in the name except Greenlawn and I'm not even sure if it's on Long Island."

"No, she's pretty adamant. 'Green' is definitely in the name."

"I just don't know."

"Field," Mary Ann said.

"Field green?"

"No, a green field."

"Wait. Is she not buried in a cemetery? Was she murdered? Is she in some green field somewhere?"

"A green field, a green field," Mary Ann kept repeating to herself. "Wait," she had called out. "Greenfield is the name of the cemetery."

"Greenfield?"

"Yes, Greenfield."

"Are you sure? And it's around here?"

"That's what she's saying."

"I don't know, Mary Ann. I've lived around here most of my life and my grandfather was a grave digger and I never, ever heard of Greenfield Cemetery."

"Well, she's saying it exists and it's close to your house."

"What else is she saying?"

"I don't know, she just left."

Mary Ann and I talked for a few minutes about what the next steps were. Smudge one more time in the next couple of days and then call her back for further instructions.

I went downstairs and walked into the toy room and turned on the computer. I waited a moment for it to boot and wondered where the ghosts had gone. Could they just teleport to another place in the blink of an eye? Or did they walk through the door and go outside for fresh air? Where does a ghost go, anyway, when it's not haunting a house?

I did a Google search for Greenfield Cemetery and New York, convinced that there would be no match.

"Oh my God," I said out loud. There it was—Greenfield Cemetery. I clicked on the link and it was only five miles away from my house.

"Grace," I called out, "you're not going to believe this."

Chapter 12

Greenfield Cemetery is located on Nassau Road in Union-dale, New York, only seven miles from historic Roose-velt Field, where Charles Lindbergh began his legendary first solo transatlantic flight on May 20, 1927. At the time, people thought Lindbergh possessed superhuman strength and will-power to endure the thirty-seven-hour flight alone in the darkness and the frigid cold. Yet, his time in the plane may not have been as solitary as many believed. It would be twenty-five years before he told of the spirits that helped him along the way in his book *The Spirit of St. Louis*:

> These phantoms speak with human voices—friendly,
> vapor-like shapes, without substance, able to vanish or

appear at will, to pass in and out through the walls of the fuselage as though no walls were there. Now, many are crowded behind me. Now, only a few remain. First one and then another presses forward to my shoulder to speak above the engine's noise, and then draws back among the group behind. At times, voices come out of the air itself, clear yet far away, traveling through distances that can't be measured by the scale of human miles, familiar voices, conversing and advising on my flight, discussing problems of my navigation, reassuring me, giving me messages of importance unattainable in ordinary life.

Roosevelt Field is now home to a two-million-square-foot shopping mall, while nearby Uniondale is a middle-class neighborhood, made up primarily of African-American and Latino families. The cemetery is on the south side of the town and runs the length of several blocks. As I turned into the driveway I could see statues of saints and angels, and I wondered if Lindbergh's phantoms looked anything like these.

After I told Grace last night about my conversation with Mary Ann, I was feeling a lot like Freddie Jones from *Scooby-Doo*. Eventually I convinced her to be my Daphne and come with me on an investigation.

"What do we do with the kids?"

"Bring them along."

And just as my family did to me, I did to my family, a weekend outing to a local cemetery.

I pulled into the parking lot next to the administrative building. Grace said she wanted to wait outside with the boys, and I left the car and walked to the office.

Inside, the place was decorated in old wood paneling from the '60s and '70s and a faded industrial rug. The place was clean and quiet and a man with white hair and a white beard asked if he could help me.

"Yes, I'm trying to find some information about someone buried here. Do you have any Boxes buried here?" Before I finished my sentence I knew what I had said.

"Oh, we have plenty of boxes," the man said, rolling his eyes. A laugh broke out from the corner of the office, where a woman in glasses was typing at the computer.

"That's good, really. No, I mean, do you have anyone named Box here. Last name Box. It's an unusual name and I never ever heard anyone with a name like that."

"Oh, there are a lot of Boxes buried here," the woman in the corner called out. She was in her late forties, with long, straight blond hair, small eyes, and glasses. "It used to be a popular name."

The man pulled out a pencil and a piece of paper and asked, "Okay, so when did he die?"

"It's a she."

"When did *she* die," the man said, rolling his eyes.

"I don't know. Turn of the century, maybe."

"What, like 2000?"

"No, no. Sorry. Like 1900. Sometime around there."

He walked over to a floor-to-ceiling revolving file cabinet. He pressed a button and a huge medieval-looking contraption started to spin like a Ferris wheel and then stopped. I wondered if they had a Cold War bomb shelter in another room.

"First name?"

"I don't know."

"You don't know the first name?" He put his hand on his hip and cocked his head. If he had been packing heat, I'm sure he would have said, "Reach for the sky, smart-ass." Instead, he asked, "What's going on here?"

I didn't know what he meant by that. Did he think I was part of some satanic cult or looking for a name to create a phony American Express card?

Shaking my head, I said, "Look, you wouldn't believe me if I told you. Can you just tell me if there have been any women named Box buried here in the late 1800s, early 1900s?"

He started riffling through index cards, stopping at times to peer at a name and a date. After a minute or two, he looked up and said, "So you want a woman, right?"

"Yes, that's right."

"All right then you don't want this one, I just came

across a little girl, a one-year-old named Clara Box. Died on March 7, 1927."

Gooseflesh covered my body and I felt for a brief moment like I was going to pass out. "Come again?" I said.

"Clara Box. One year old. Died on March 7, 1927." And he put the card back in the file.

"Wait. Can you put that one aside?"

"Why? You said you were looking for a woman."

"Well, yeah, but, let's just put that one aside and we'll come back to it," I said to him and asked him to keep looking.

I felt like I was under a spell. Another minute passed. I felt my palms starting to sweat and I looked around the room feeling nervous and anxious. Is this all some crazy coincidence or is there something else going on? Is this little girl somehow related to the woman who passed away?

Then I heard words that brought me back to earth. "I think I found what you're looking for. Here it is. Hannah Box. Died 1899."

THE MAN WROTE DOWN all the information for me. I thanked him, and as I was about to leave, he asked me, "Can you tell me what you're doing?" I walked back and began to tell him the story and realized by the time I was done, almost a half-hour had passed.

"That March 7 thing is pretty strange," he said.

"I just don't know what it means."

Then the blond-haired woman, who had been listening to the story, called out from across the room, "You're not going to believe this, but I got married on March 7. And you don't want to know how that turned out."

Chapter 13

A guardian angel is "a celestial spirit assigned by God to watch over each individual during life," John Hardon says. Its role is "both to guide and guard; to guide as a messenger of God's will to our minds, and to guard as an instrument of God's goodness in protecting us from evil." But what happens when someone dies? Does that protector follow them into eternal life?

There was a statue of a guardian angel holding a flower in its right hand about thirty feet from the Box gravesite. With its wings outstretched, this androgynous stone sentinel overlooked Nassau Road. Its eyes were turned down so it couldn't see Marco's Auto Body Shop, the day care center next door, or the thousands of cars that drive down the busy street every day. Angels, being pure spirit, probably have no need for eyes, but standing below the statue you can feel its gaze, watching, observing, and praying for the living and the dead.

I stood there in the cemetery next to Grace. She was holding Charlie in her arms and I was holding Eddie's hand. We walked over to where Hannah's tombstone should have been, but only found a small obelisk engraved with the names of a number of Box family members. There was George and Maria Box, and there was Jennie, who had died in 1899. She seemed to be the first wife of George. No trace of a Hannah anywhere.

We drove to another part of the cemetery and spent a half-hour looking at old weathered tombstones in search of Clara Box, who had died on March 7, eighty years earlier. She, too, couldn't be found. On our way home, I stopped back at the administrative office and the man behind the counter apologized for not telling me that the little girl never had a marker. He did reassure us that Hannah did, but by that point my kids were getting restless and Grace was tired, so we left and I took them all to her mother's.

I went back home, thinking about all the people at Greenfield Cemetery and how the dead are soon forgotten by subsequent generations. I would think about my grandfather often and visit him throughout the year at his resting place in Calverton National Cemetery, but I rarely, if ever, thought of his father or his father's father. They weren't even memories to me.

I smudged the house one more time, as Mary Ann suggested, and nothing strange happened. Later that afternoon I called her to give an update and to let her know that I had found a woman named Hannah Box but couldn't find her tombstone.

"She's right here now, honey," Mary Ann said. "She says you're right and wrong."

"What does that mean?"

"She's saying her name is Hannah Jane, but people always called her Jennie."

MARY ANN AND I TALKED for a little while longer. I told her about the little girl, Clara Box, and the strange correlation with March 7, but she couldn't offer an explanation. "I just see ghosts, honey. I'm not a numerologist."

"Could we ask Jennie if they're related?"

"We could, but she's not here anymore."

"You mean for good?"

"No, but I think she's getting ready to go."

"And Peter?"

"He's not there, either. They don't like the smudging and I think he's ready to go, too."

The house seemed quieter than it had in a very long time and as we talked on the phone, I walked back and forth between the rooms upstairs. I knew that this was all drawing to a close and even though I was happy, there was a part of me that couldn't help feeling melancholy about it all as well.

"Hey, can we just get rid of Peter and keep Mrs. Box?" I asked.

"No, honey. They don't belong here. It's time for them to move on."

I felt like I was going to cry, and I wondered how many people living today ever thought about Hannah Jane "Jennie" Box. And I wondered how long before the people who knew Peter Smith would forget the shape of his face or the sound of his voice. One of Grace's biggest fears was forgetting the way her father had laughed, and from time to time I would come downstairs and see her watching old videos from some relative's wedding. Her father was camera shy, but occasionally the camera would pan across a room and catch him whispering something in his wife's ear. Grace wishes she knew what he said.

"Okay, Mary Ann. What do I have to do next?"

"Do you live near a funeral home?"

"Well, as a matter of fact, I do. There's one literally across the street."

"Really? Oh, I bet you've had a lot of visitors over the years. Every earthbound spirit visits their own wake and funeral, but just like regular people they get bored after a while and move about."

"Great, so this place is like a magnet?"

"You have two ghosts in your house, so what do you think?"

"Good point."

I told Mary Ann about some of the weird dreams I had had over the years and asked if she thought the two ghosts in the house had been responsible for them. She doubted it and said that there were other spirits besides the earthbound who could, or would, do such a thing. "As much as you may have upset the man ghost, he was probably trying to get your attention the night you felt like you couldn't breathe. He was probably trying to protect you."

I listened to her words and more questions rolled around in my head. Do dark spirits haunt ghosts if they get stuck in-between this world and the next? Can an earthbound spirit communicate directly with angels? Were ghosts ever in danger from other spirits? Had Jennie and Peter been guarding our house all along and would we miss them when they were gone? And what would happen to them once they crossed over?

I didn't ask any of these things though. Instead, all I said was, "I guess this is it, then."

"Okay, honey, this is what you do."

Chapter 14

For over a week, we waited for someone to die.

Mary Ann said that I was lucky to live so close to a funeral home because when someone dies they are surrounded by the white light, which acts as a doorway to the other side. The white light, however, gets dimmer as time goes on and if a spirit doesn't walk into it within seventy-two hours, give or take a day, then a spirit can grow confused and become stuck. Usually, spirits depart at the funeral service or when the family is standing around at the gravesite.

Mary Ann's instructions were to briefly explain to the ghosts what was happening, but not engage them further—"You are going to cross over"—and then walk them over to the funeral home with instructions to go inside, find the white light, and go into it.

Now, people must drop like flies in Rockville Centre. Macken Mortuary was always doing steady business and it seemed that just about every day there was a funeral service going on across the street. So the plan was to walk Jennie and Peter over the next day and to bring our haunting to a close. But the next day arrived and there was no one at the funeral home. Nor the next day, nor the next.

The following Monday, more than a week after Mary Ann gave me my marching orders, there was still no funeral service at the mortuary.

"Are you freaking kidding me?" I said to Grace in the kitchen while Eddie was playing with a Frosty the Snowman doll in the other room. "You mean to tell me that no one is dying in Rockville Centre anymore?"

Upon hearing this, Grace had closed her eyes, covered her ears with her hands, and said, "Haven't you learned to watch what you say?"

She was right. She was always right. But the house was starting to feel unsettled again and I didn't want to have to go through the process of smudging one more time. It had been a long couple of weeks. It had been a long year. And I just wanted to have some resolution.

Later that evening, after Eddie and Charlie fell asleep in

our room, Grace and I were carrying laundry up the stairs to the second floor. As Grace crossed the threshold of Eddie's room, the lightbulb popped. Grace screamed and dropped the clothes to the floor.

"Why the hell did the light go out?"

As she said this, I felt something like a breeze blow past me, but I didn't tell her that.

"You're going to wake the kids. It's nothing," I said. "It's just a lightbulb. They blow out all the time." I thought I sounded pretty convincing, but I wasn't 100 percent sure that we had finally hit the 700th hour of the lightbulb's life.

"I'm so tired of all this shit," she said. "I just want it to stop."

I put my basket down, helped her pick up the clothes, and then heard something that sounded a lot like a small chain saw coming from downstairs.

Grace stood up and tried to figure out where it was coming from and whispered loudly to me, "What is *that*?"

"I don't know. I don't know." I raced down the stairs, turned the corner, and followed the sound, which was coming from the kitchen. I stopped for a second before I entered, trying to make out what it could be, and that's when I saw it. I had bought an electric toothbrush the week before and kept it downstairs because I didn't want it to wake the kids when I used it in the morning. (I was still getting up early every morning to pray and write.) It was buzzing in its charger. "Weird," I said to myself as I walked over to switch it off.

Grace came back downstairs. "It was my toothbrush," I said.

"It just went off by itself?"

"I don't know. Yeah, I think so."

"Are we safe here? Are the kids okay?"

"Yeah. I mean, I don't know what's happening, but if Mary Ann felt like we were in danger, she would have said so."

The two of us walked into the living room, sat down, and after a few moments we switched on the TV and tried to relax. The room was a mess. Ed's stuffed animals were all over the floor, but neither of us had enough strength to get up and put them away. As we sat there, Eddie's Frosty the Snowman doll began to sing his song:

Frosty the snowman was a jolly happy soul.

"No shit," I said.

Grace just shook her head. "I told you to watch what you say."

"I'm sorry, I'm sorry."

"You have this gift for royally pissing off people at the most inopportune time and now you've gone and pissed off some ghosts."

. . .

As I was walking home from the train station the next day, I saw a person walk out of Macken Mortuary, get into her car, and drive away. I ran home as fast as I could, swung open the door and called out to Grace, "Okay, they're going."

"Who's going?" Eddie said to me.

"Ah, nobody. Nobody is going anywhere."

Grace looked at me like I was crazy.

"There's people across the street," I said.

"So this is it?"

"I think so."

I ran upstairs into Eddie's room and closed the door and talked to the air.

"Okay, Peter and Jennie, you have to come with me." I gave them the instructions Mary Ann had given me. I then opened the door, went down the stairs, told Grace and Eddie that I would be right back, and walked across the street to the front door of the funeral home.

"This is where we say so long. There's going to be a white light inside; the two of you need to go into it. I promise I'll pray for you. I'll always pray for you." And there on the steps of a funeral home I said the Our Father and prayed they would have a safe passage to wherever it was they were going.

I turned and left them there. As I made my way to the end of the walkway, I heard the door open behind me.

"Can I help you?" one of the funeral directors called to me.

What I wanted to say was, "Gee sir, I was hoping to help a couple ghosts over the River Styx and thought you could be of some assistance," but all I could muster up was, "Yes, I just wanted to see if you were open."

"We're open."

"Good," I said and walked home. I called Mary Ann that night and told her it was done. I also mentioned to her all the weird things that had happened the night before: the light-bulb, the electric toothbrush, the Frosty the Snowman doll.

"Oh, honey, they were ready to go. They were just trying to say good-bye."

THE NEXT MORNING, I woke up and heard something I had never heard before. Quiet. In all my years of living in the house, I had never heard quiet quite like I heard it the morning after Jennie Box and Peter Smith crossed over. It was as if a giant white noise machine had been on since I first moved in when I was six years old and someone had just turned it off. It was five o'clock and, instead of getting up and praying downstairs like I normally did, I lay in bed, kept my promise, and prayed for the souls of the departed.

A few days later, I was walking home from work a little later than usual and saw a steady stream of people filing into

Macken Mortuary. The street was abuzz with activity. Car doors slammed, women in high heels were adjusting skirts, a group of teenage boys in button-down shirts and ties were smoking under a tree. Some girls were laughing with their boyfriends. Older people dressed in black held their heads low. Some people were crying.

I didn't know who died, but I heard someone say it was sad that *he* passed away so suddenly. So it was a man, someone's son, possibly a brother or father. It was obvious he knew a lot of people. As I walked by, I imagined his spirit standing by the foot of his coffin, watching friends and relatives as they paid their last respects. I offered a prayer to the nameless man and wished him as much love in the next life as he seemed to have experienced in this one.

Walking home in the light of early evening, the world looked different to me—the way it does when you fall in love or lose someone close to you. John Hardon defined a miracle as an event "surpassing at least the powers of visible nature, produced by God to witness to some truth or testify to someone's sanctity." If that's the case, then the last year hadn't been a haunting, but a miracle unfolding. The truth is, no one knows the mind of God, and the greatest challenge to faith is realizing that nothing happens without the Almighty's stamp of approval—good or bad. It is the great mystery of belief and learning to accept that can take a lifetime—and sometimes more than that. But, there is holiness in everything and sometimes we need to be spooked to see that. I had been given a glimpse of an unseen world. I couldn't see ghosts and I couldn't hear angels. But then, for that matter, I couldn't see ultraviolet rays, either. That didn't mean they didn't exist or didn't have some influence in our lives. My mom knew this better than anyone.

As I opened the front door, I called out hello and heard Grace and Eddie upstairs. They both giggled down to me and said that Charlie had been laughing at something and threw up milk through his nose and they were cleaning him up. I walked upstairs and as I reached the landing I turned to my left and saw the three of them in Eddie's bedroom.

I looked at them standing in the yellow room with no closets, and as I stepped over the threshold, Eddie ran over and wrapped his arms around my legs.

"He missed you," Grace said. "We all did."

"I missed you, too," I said.

I gave Grace a look. She smiled and shrugged her shoulders and said, "Eddie woke up this morning and the first thing he wanted to do was play in his room."

Acknowledgments

I could not be more fortunate than to have Mitch Horowitz as my editor on this project. His vision, advice, patience, and friendship were impeccable. He made me laugh. He made me think. He made me a better writer and in the end a better person, too. My deepest gratitude for everything you've done for me, Mitch.

Nor could I be more privileged than to work with all the wonderful people at the Penguin Group and Tarcher. Thank you to Gabrielle Moss, whose professionalism and sense of humor helped shepherd this book through all its various stages, and to Joel Fotinos, whose leadership helped make this book happen. Thank you to Bonnie Soodek, Brianna

Yamashita, Lauren Reddy, Lisa D'Agostino, and David Walker for all your hard work and guidance. And special thanks to all my old friends down on Hudson Street, including Kathryn Court, Sabila Khan, Lance Fitzgerald, Leigh Butler, Hal Fessenden, Melanie Koch, and Kelli Daniel-Richards. I worked with many of you for years while I was at the book clubs and I can't even begin to tell you how exciting it has been for me to work with you as an author. Thank you for all your guidance and warmth over the years. I truly am blessed to have crossed paths with all of you.

Thank you to Mary Ann and Ted Winkowski for all your love and kindheartedness. Mary Ann, I've said this before, but I'll say it again, you really changed the way I see the world in wonderful ways and I feel so blessed to know you. Thank you for all you support and for fielding all my questions with patience and humor.

A big thanks to my agent, Victoria Skurnick, for being one of my greatest supporters and one of my dearest friends. Thank you for all the encouragement you've given me over the years.

Thank you to Father Michael Holleran. You only came into my life a few months ago, but I feel like I've known you forever. Thank you for the great talks, for your expert advice about the spirit world, and for guiding me through it.

Thank you to Jennifer Stallone Riddell for your insight, humor, and friendship. Thank you for reading this book through its various stages and rallying me toward the finish line. You truly are one of the greats.

Thank you to Gilles Dana for believing in my voice.

Thank you to Anne-Marie Rutella for all your love and friendship over the years and helping me copyedit this book before my delivery date. You were under the gun and your meticulousness was much appreciated. A special shout out to Anthony I, Anthony II, and Aisling.

Thank you to Noelle Kuchler for being a great friend and for all your questions which helped me considerably in forming this book. I couldn't have done this without you.

Thank you to Loretta Holmes for your enthusiasm and inspiration. You have been one of my greatest supporters over the years. Your life has changed my life.

Thank you to Deborah Sinclaire for championing this book, for your friendship, and for all the laughs over the years.

Thank you to Eric Hafker and Michael Stephenson. You are two of the greatest men who ever lived and two of my dearest friends. Thank you for all the love, laughs, poetry, foul talk, and all the wine. Special thanks to you, Eric, for helping me out in the very last stages of this book. I'm so happy your eyes read these pages when they did.

Thank you to Darya Porat, Talia Krohn, John Burke, my friends and colleagues, for all your graciousness and encouragement. You've all been great to me.

Thank you to Trace Murphy for your kindness, patience, friendship—and for telling great stories.

Thank you to the following for their dedication, support, and friendship: Cindy Karamitis, Erin Locke, Matt Baglio, Becky Cabaza, Charlie Conrad, Jenna Ciongoli, Deb Sabatino, Brandy Flora, Maria Schulz, Tanya Twerdowsky Sylvan, Kristine Puopolo, Tricia Wygal, Amy Boorstein, Therese Borchard, Jay Franco, Carol Mackey, Jessie Bright, Ryan Buell, Greg Kincaid, Jon Sweeney, Tom Craughwell, Steve Irby, Richard and Joy Newcombe, John Taylor, Kelsey Amble, Brian and Lisa McCarthy, Laurie Balut, Jeannine and Brad Dillon, Sam Honen, Joan Louise Brookbank, Jennifer Walsh, Ray Casazza, Beth Goehring, Sharon Fantera, Larry Shapiro, Laura Balducci, Cynthia Clarke, Doreen Sinski, John "The Sarge" Miller, Raquel Avila, Liz Kirmss, Jean Bjork, Steve Scarallo, Anthony Cole, Jill Fabiani, Patricia Clement, Pam Fitzgerald, Ellen Giesow, Karen Strejlau, Amalia Buendia, Michael and Fran Bartholomew, Nancy Schleyer, Maria Theresa Gutierrez, Janet Shavel, Kathy Vella, Robert and Maureen Sullivan, Marc Vital-Herne, Estelle Peck, Patricia Schreck, Maddalena Pennino, Jennifer Kanakos, Sandy Strk, Susan Stalzer, Audrey Puzzo, Michael Palgon, Lisa Thornbloom, Jessica Walles, Kalyani Fernando, Eric Zagrans, Patrick Coleman, Clark Strand, Maria Tahim, Kathy Viele, Alexander Shaia, James Philipps, Maura Zagrans,

Jennifer Puglisi, Audrey and Alex Robles, Johnny and Elvira Diaz, Rosemary Ellen Guiley, and my friend Peggy.

Thank you to Will "Sticks" Romano. We've been friends for over twenty years and you are an endless fountain of inspiration for me. God bless you, man!

Thank you to Frances, Josephine, Lenny, and Carrie Poppi for all your love, patience, direction and kindness over the years. I couldn't be luckier to call you family.

Thanks to all the folks at Panera in Rockville Centre, New York, especially Christian Alexandre. Thank you again for your kindness and for always remembering my name and for the delicious coffee that woke me up on those early mornings when I would write by the window that overlooked Merrick Road.

Thank you to Annie Leuenberger for all the ghost stories and for your enduring friendship and love over the years. You are, and always will be, one of the greats in my life.

Thank you to Michael "Leo" McCormack for your healthy skepticism, your humor, your loyalty, and all the Guinness. I am proud to call you Leo.

Thank you to Courtney Snyder for your enduring friendship and for inspiring me when I most need it.

Thank you to Jessica Rey for all your inspiration and for changing my life. God bless you and your family.

Thank you to Debbie Marzigliano, who helped in the research for this book.

Thank you to my mom for all your love and support on this project. You are the most courageous person I know and I'm proud to be your son.

Thank you to my sisters Annie, Mary, Suzie, and Julie for all the memories and love. You are all blessings to me.

Thanks to my dad, wherever you may be.

As always, thank you to the loves of my life, Grace, Eddie, and Charlie. Grace, you were wonderful for putting up with me over the last years as I pulled this work together and you continue to surprise and inspire me every day. Eddie and Charlie, my goodness, words can't even describe how honored I am to know the two of you.

And last, this book is especially dedicated to the memory of Bert Poppi, Christopher Gruhn, Peter Smith, Hannah Jane "Jennie" Box, Clara Box, and to my grandparents Julia and Harry Powell, who loved me like a son and were two of my greatest champions.

About the Author

Gary Jansen has worked in publishing for more than fifteen years and served as editor in chief of Quality Paperback Book Club. He is currently an editor at the Crown Publishing Group, specializing in books on religion and spirituality. His first book, *The Rosary: A Journey to the Beloved*, was praised by Paulo Coelho, the bestselling author of *The Alchemist*, as "a wonderful book. Not just wonderful, but very important." Publishers Weekly's review of Jansen's second book, *Exercising Your Soul: Fifteen Minutes a Day to a Spiritual Life*, called him an author who "amuses and inspires." Both books were published by Faithwords/Hachette. Jansen lives in New York with his wife and two sons.